PLANT BASED COOKBOOK

D1363560

GOOD FOR YOUR HEART, YOUR HEALTH, AND YOUR LIFE

Contents

Introduction

Colorful vegetables, sweet fruit, hearty whole grains, nutritional nuts and seeds, protein-rich beans and legumes—these are just a few of the wholesome whole foods you'll enjoy on a plant-based diet.

The benefits of a plant-based diet are as plentiful and varied as the food you'll eat. And it's no coincidence that prominent physicians such as Dr. Dean Ornish, president and founder of the nonprofit Preventive Medicine Research Institute, as well as Clinical Professor of Medicine at the University of California; Dr. Kim Williams, distinguished cardiologist, professor of medicine, and president-elect of the American College of Cardiology; and many others cite a plant-based diet as the key to reversing heart disease and the aging process, lowering cholesterol, and promoting overall good health and longevity.

Plant-Based Cookbook was designed to empower you to embrace a diet full of fresh and healthy plant-based foods. In these 200 recipes—for breakfasts, sauces, salad dressings, dips, sandwiches, soups, one-pot meals, casseroles, satisfying meat substitutes, breads, pastas, and more—you'll find inspiration from many cultures and cuisines, plus new and familiar flavors that will help you transition. And of course, there are plenty of desserts, too! You'll also find new culinary techniques, tips for making recipes in advance, and instructions for freezing dishes when applicable.

I encourage you to take these recipes and make them your own. Experiment, have fun, and enjoy the journey to a happier, healthier, plant-based you.

 ### Making the Transition

Transitioning to a plant-based diet in a way that's comfortable for you is important, and this book offers strategies to help you make positive changes in your diet without missing meat and dairy. If you aren't ready to completely give up animal-based food, begin by making small changes, and use this book to help you gradually replace the meat, dairy, and eggs in your favorite recipes with plant ingredients. Try plant-based milk in your morning coffee. Cook a few extra vegetable dishes each week, and enjoy them with smaller portions of familiar foods. Prepare some of the tempting recipes in this book—especially those marked with the "transition" icon. And always eat a big salad, every day.

 ### Just One Hour

It takes less than an hour to prepare a healthy, from-scratch, plant-based meal that leaves you feeling sated, energized, and simply fantastic. To help you get a healthy meal on the table quickly, look for the "under 30 minutes" icon on recipes throughout the book.

Other Dietary Considerations

In addition to the "transition" and "under 30 minutes" icons, the recipes are also flagged for a few other dietary considerations. Here's what to look for:

 Gluten free   Soy free

 Nut free   Good source of protein

A Note About the Recipes

I use a gas range and oven, and that's what I used when I wrote the recipes in this book. Your kitchen appliances may be faster or slower, hotter or cooler than mine. Each recipe in this book was extensively tested, so if the recipe instructions say to heat food at medium-high heat, and you feel like it might burn at that temperature on your own stovetop, adjust the heat accordingly. An inexpensive oven thermometer can tell you if your oven runs true to temperature. Every stove has its own personality and quirks, so learn to trust your instincts.

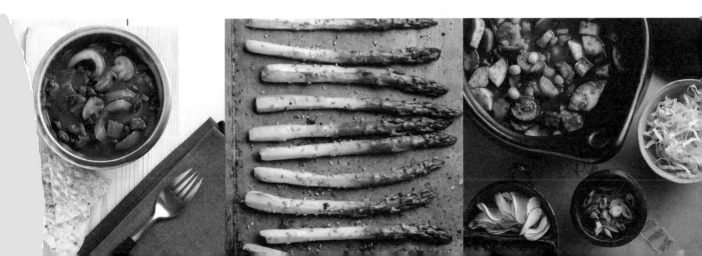

Beginning a Plant-Based Diet

Transitioning to a plant-based diet might seem intimidating, but it needn't be. Start by making small changes; explore transition strategies, cooking techniques, and meal plans; and stock your pantry with good foods, and you're off to a healthy start.

What Is a Plant-Based Diet?

A plant-based diet focuses on foods that come from plants—vegetables, fruits, whole grains, nuts, seeds, beans, and legumes—while avoiding those that come from animal sources, including meat, dairy, eggs, and food ingredients derived from animal sources like honey and gelatin.

Healthy and unhealthy choices still abound in the world of plant-based foods, though. It's entirely possible to make unhealthy choices when eating plant-based. Whole foods in their natural state are a much better choice than a processed meal from a supermarket freezer or fast-food restaurant, so choose wisely and be mindful.

Why Choose Plants?

People choose to transition to a plant-based diet for many reasons—to improve health, increase energy, treat and prevent disease, or lose weight, to name just a few. The following list may provide you with the inspiration you need to go plant-based.

A plant-based diet is healthy. Many cardiologists recommend the plant-based diet for its ability to prevent and even reverse heart disease. The plant-based diet also has been repeatedly linked to cancer prevention, weight loss, maintaining healthy intestinal flora, treating diseases such as Parkinson's and multiple sclerosis, eye diseases, diabetes, and a host of other ailments.

A plant-based diet is beautiful. Who wouldn't want healthier skin, a slimmer waistline, and a whole lot more energy? Switching to a healthy, plant-based diet that relies on fresh, whole foods leaves you looking and feeling fantastic.

A plant-based diet is youthful. A 2013 study by the Preventive Medicine Research Institute and the University of California, San Francisco, cited the plant-based diet as a key factor in reversing the aging process. Study participants who adopted a plant-based diet (and exercised regularly) showed a 10 percent lengthening of telomeres (the protective ends of DNA strands), which results in longer cell life. By contrast, the participants who continued on an animal-based diet shortened their telomeres by 3 percent. According to Dr. Dean Ornish, who led this groundbreaking study, "Shortened telomeres have been shown to play a role in heart disease, colon cancer, stroke, dementia, and premature death."

A plant-based diet is sustainable. According to the United Nations' 2005 Millennium Ecosystem Assessment, agriculture, particularly meat and dairy products, accounts for 70 percent of global freshwater consumption, 38 percent of total land use, and 19 percent of the world's greenhouse gas emissions. Livestock farming is linked to antibiotic resistance, water pollution, and a host of other environmental catastrophes.

A plant-based diet is clean. In addition to antibiotic usage, the meat industry is rife with disease. Increasingly, we see food recalls due to contamination of meat, resulting in outbreaks of illness from potentially deadly food-borne bacteria.

What Do You Eat?

It's easy to eat a plant-based diet. Simply choose a wide variety of fresh, colorful fruits and vegetables, including plenty of dark, leafy greens. Add protein from sources such as beans, legumes, and meat analogs, and fill in with healthy fats from nuts, seeds, and avocados.

PLANT-BASED FOOD GROUP	EXAMPLES	WHAT IT PROVIDES
FRUITS AND VEGETABLES	Apples, avocados, bananas, berries, broccoli, brussels sprouts, cauliflower, citrus fruits, eggplant, kale, pears, root vegetables, spinach, tomatoes, winter squash, zucchini	A broad spectrum of vital nutrients, fiber, protein, antioxidants, micronutrients, healthy carbohydrates, calcium, magnesium, potassium, iron, beta-carotene, vitamin B complex, vitamin C, vitamin A, and vitamin K
BEANS AND LEGUMES	Cannellini beans, chickpeas, flageolets, kidney beans, lentils, peas, soybeans	Protein, fiber, antioxidants, vitamins, low-glycemic healthy carbohydrates, B vitamins, calcium, potassium, folate
WHOLE GRAINS	Amaranth, brown rice, cornmeal, couscous, farro, millet, quinoa (actually a seed), wheat berries, whole-wheat flour	Fiber, protein, healthy carbohydrates (whole grains), B vitamins, antioxidants, iron, magnesium
NUTS AND SEEDS	Almonds, Brazil nuts, cashews, chia seeds, flaxseeds, pecans, pumpkin seeds, sunflower seeds, walnuts	Healthy fats, fiber, protein, magnesium, zinc, calcium, phosphorus
MEAT ANALOGS	Organic tofu, seitan, tempeh	Protein, familiar flavors, and meatlike textures to make transitioning easy

Transition Strategies

Transitioning to a plant-based diet doesn't have to be difficult. With a little planning, it's easy to get all the nutrients you need from plant sources without relying on processed, refined foods—and without feeling like you're missing out on anything.

Start with Small Changes

For many, the transition to a plant-based diet is gradual. Observing a "meatless Monday" is a great way to start. Begin with one plant-based meal a day and then move on to two meals a day. Start eliminating the worst offenders from your diet, such as bacon and cheese, and have a fresh vegetable dish or two with every meal.

Eat Your Veggies

The additional fiber in a plant-based diet can be a shock to the system for those accustomed to unhealthy processed foods; large quantities of meat; and few, if any, fresh vegetables, fruits, and whole grains. A gradual increase in your fiber intake can be beneficial if you're prone to digestive disturbance.

Start by eating a big, raw salad every day. Increase the amount of beans, legumes, fruits, and vegetables you eat, while decreasing or eliminating meat, dairy, and eggs.

Vegetable Enchiladas with Roasted Tomato Sauce
Tomatoes, onions, zucchini, corn, black beans, and peppers meld with plant-based cheese in this zesty comfort dish.

Have a Plan

If you're new to the plant-based lifestyle, you'll want to do some meal planning. Planning your meals, and maybe doing a little cooking on your day off, can eliminate the urge to backslide into unhealthy eating. You'll be less likely to give in and order that sausage and pepperoni pizza if you've shopped for healthy ingredients or have a veggie casserole in the freezer ready to pop into the oven when you're hungry but don't have a lot of time.

Seek Inspiration

Websites, magazines, blogs, cookbooks—inspiration is out there for those who seek it. Don't be afraid to try new things. The worst that can happen is you won't like a dish or meal.

I find that the foods and techniques I've come to love the most are those I resisted making because I thought I didn't have enough time, or I assumed I wouldn't like the end result. Try something new a few times a week, add the dishes you love to your repertoire, and forget the rest.

Hearty Chilli

Iman Bayildi

Go Faux!

Miss the meat? A whole world
of meat substitutes is out there, waiting for you to sample,
from Tofurky to "veggie" pepperoni. I don't advocate
eating these processed foods every day, but they do help
satisfy cravings for familiar foods. And who doesn't want a
little soy chorizo or a grilled veggie dog in their life once in
a while?

Explore New Frontiers

The plant-based diet is a great opportunity to boldly go
where you've not gone before. Whether you visit an
Indian vegetarian restaurant or gather your friends to
create a Middle Eastern meze, you'll find that many
cuisines throughout the world rely on very little (or even
no) meat, with vegetables and whole grains forming the
bulk of the meal.

The "peasant cuisine" of the Italian countryside my
grandmother favored included vegetables grown in the
garden, a salad at every meal, plenty of fresh bread, hearty
soups, and stews spooned over hot and satisfying polenta.
You'll find recipes throughout this book that rely on that
tradition as well as ones that explore cuisines you might
not be familiar with. Be daring, and jump on in!

Move at Your Own Pace

Finally, adopting a plant-based diet is all about the
journey, and each of us experiences that journey
differently. Open your mind and heart, and commit to
seeking health and happiness through your diet.

Challenges will present themselves—when you're
traveling, when you're a guest in someone else's home, or
when you're just plain tired and hungry and tempted by
the familiar. When you fall, dust yourself off and start over.

Any change for the better is a good thing. Give
yourself a break, and do the best you can.

Filling Your Plant-Based Pantry

When stocking your plant-based pantry, focus on healthy, whole foods in their natural, unprocessed state. In addition, try some of the specialty foods and ingredients that can make cooking fun and tasty.

Vegetables
Choose a wide array of fresh and frozen vegetables like salad greens; leafy greens such as collards or kale; mushrooms; cruciferous vegetables such as cauliflower and cabbage; and aromatics like onions, carrots, and celery. Frozen vegetables can be a nutritious alternative to fresh, and in-season vegetables from a local farm are more economical and flavorful. I stock my freezer with broccoli, peas, greens, and corn from the farmers' market.

Fruits
Fresh fruits such as bananas, berries, apples, and pears are great to eat as is or to use in baked dishes. Frozen fruits are fantastic in smoothies and pies, and you should always keep a stock of peeled, ripe bananas in the freezer for baking emergencies.

Beans and Legumes
Choose a variety of dried and canned beans and legumes to provide an inexpensive, easy-to-cook protein source. I keep lentils, chickpeas, black beans, kidney beans, and cannellini beans in my pantry. Many recipes in this book call for canned beans because that's what most busy cooks rely on to get dinner on the table. Don't be afraid to cook dry beans from scratch though—it's easy and economical.

Grains
Keep a variety of grains and grainlike seeds on hand, such as brown rice, basmati rice, cornmeal, whole-wheat pastry flour, all-purpose flour, whole-wheat and semolina pasta, rolled oats, barley, millet, farro, couscous, rice noodles, and quinoa. If you follow a gluten-free diet, almond flour, gluten-free flour mix, and oat flour are wonderful additions to your pantry.

Oils and Vinegars

Start with a good extra-virgin olive oil and a neutral-flavored oil such as grapeseed. Coconut oil is great in curries and baked goods. Nut oils add flavor to baked goods and salad dressings, and toasted sesame oil brings a smoky, nutty flavor. Refrigerate oils you don't use every day. Apple cider vinegar, red wine vinegar, and balsamic vinegar provide plenty of versatility. Rice vinegar is fabulous in Asian recipes, while umeboshi plum vinegar brings a unique salty, sour, pungent flavor to dishes.

Nuts and Seeds

Stash raw almonds and cashews in the pantry for baking, making "cheese" fillings and nut milks, and plain old snacking. Walnuts and pecans make everything more delicious, especially when toasted. Chia and flaxseeds are essential to the plant-based baking pantry and can be added to salads, fruit dishes, breads, and oatmeal. Roasted, salted pumpkin seeds (pepitas) are nice, too. Store nuts and seeds in tightly sealed glass jars, and freeze seldom-used ingredients.

Soy Products

No plant-based pantry is complete without tofu, tempeh, edamame, and miso. Tofu absorbs the flavor of what it's cooked with, making it ideal in curries and stews. Tempeh, a fermented soy product, has an umami flavor and meaty texture perfect for grilling, sandwiches, and casseroles. Edamame are whole soybeans and are good in soups, stews, and salads in the same way you'd use beans. Miso is an essential ingredient when building umami flavor.

Condiments

Stock a variety of homemade and store-bought condiments to add to recipes or enjoy on cooked foods. Ketchup, hot sauce, whole-grain Dijon mustard, and plant-based mayo are essentials.

Try these spices, herbs, and seasonings to complement your plant-based diet: black pepper; cayenne; cumin; dried dill, oregano, and thyme; fresh basil, chervil, cilantro, dill, parsley, and tarragon; herbes de Provence; Himalayan black sea salt; kosher salt; nutritional yeast; sea salt (regular and smoked); smoked paprika; turmeric; and more!

Plant-Based Cooking Techniques

Plant-based cooking is easy once you master some basic techniques and equip yourself with helpful supplies: a 2-quart (2L) or more saucepan with a tight-fitting lid; a steamer basket; an assortment of mixing bowls; spoons and spatulas; some heavy, rimmed baking sheets; and a large, heavy sauté pan. A food processor is a nice extra that cuts down on prep time.

Steaming Vegetables

Steaming is a simple way to cook vegetables with maximum flavor and nutrition retention. To steam, bring several inches of water to a boil in a saucepan fitted with a steamer basket over medium-high heat. Add the vegetables, cover with the lid, and cook until the vegetables are tender. The following table lists steaming times for several vegetables.

Steaming peas
Snow peas require only 2 or 3 minutes of steaming to come out perfectly tender and crisp. Oversteaming makes them dull and soggy.

Vegetable	Steam Time
Asparagus	3 or 4 minutes
Broccoli	4 or 5 minutes
Brussels sprouts	10 minutes
Carrots	4 or 5 minutes
Cauliflower	6 minutes
Green beans	5 minutes
Hardy greens (kale, collards)	7 to 9 minutes
Peas	2 or 3 minutes

Roasting Vegetables

Roasting brings out deep flavors from root vegetables, brussels sprouts, asparagus, broccoli, and winter squash. To roast, preheat the oven to 400°F (200°C). Cut vegetables into uniform pieces, and place in a baking pan lined with parchment paper. Toss with just enough olive oil to coat; season with salt, black pepper, and dried herbs (if desired); and roast, stirring once or twice, until tender and caramelized.

Tender vegetables such as asparagus will roast to perfection in less than 10 minutes, while winter squash and potatoes need more time—up to 45 minutes. Try roasting broccoli, cauliflower, rutabaga, sweet potatoes, turnips, mushrooms, zucchini, small onions, and even green beans!

Roasted vegetables
Roasted vegetables add flavor, nutrition, and a pop of color to any meal.

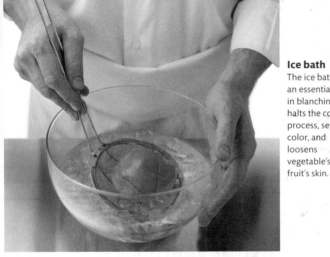

Ice bath
The ice bath is an essential step in blanching. It halts the cooking process, sets color, and loosens vegetable's or fruit's skin.

Vegetable	Blanch Time
Artichoke	7 minutes
Asparagus	2 minutes
Beans (green, snap)	2 minutes
Beans (lima, cranberry)	2 to 4 minutes
Broccoli	2 or 3 minutes
Brussels sprouts	3 minutes
Carrots	2 minutes
Cauliflower	2 or 3 minutes
Collards/kale	3 minutes

Blanching Vegetables

When you want vegetables to remain crunchy and fresh and preserve their bright green color, or if you're preparing to freeze in-season produce, you'll want to do some blanching. To blanch, bring a large pot of salted water to a boil over medium-high heat. Prepare an ice bath by filling a bowl with cold water and ice. Cut vegetables into uniform pieces, and drop in boiling water (see the following table for recommended times). Using a slotted spoon, remove the vegetables from the hot water, transfer to the ice bath, and drain in a colander or on paper towels.

Sautéed greens
Sautéing greens with a little olive oil and garlic is a quick and delicious way to get your daily serving of greens.

Sautéing Vegetables

A quick sauté lets you cook vegetables with aromatics such as onions, garlic, and herbs for fresh, fantastic flavor. To sauté, heat a small amount of fat, such as olive oil, over medium-high heat in a heavy sauté pan. Add onions, and cook for 1 or 2 minutes, stir in garlic, and cook for 1 more minute. Add vegetables to the pan, and cook, stirring frequently, just until vegetables are tender. Mushrooms, tender summer squash, broccoli, spinach, and peas are all excellent candidates for the sauté pan.

Aromatic vegetables
Aromatics such as celery, onions, and carrot add the building blocks of flavor to soups, stews, and sauces.

Cooking Rice

With the exception of Arborio rice for risotto, rinse rice before cooking it. Measure the rice, place in a large bowl, cover with cold water, and swish around with your hands to release the rice's starch and any soil. Drain and repeat three times. Place the rice in a pan with a tight-fitting lid, add water, and set over medium-high heat. Bring to a full, rolling boil, stir once, and cover. Reduce heat to the lowest setting, and cook for the time noted on the rice package. Remove from heat and let stand, covered, for 5 to 10 minutes before fluffing with a fork and serving.

Hold it
You can hold cooked rice, covered and with a clean kitchen towel under the lid, for up to 20 minutes. Fluff with a fork before serving.

Rice and water
Add rice and cold, fresh water at the same time— don't boil the water first.

Cooking Pasta

Cook pasta in several quarts of boiling water, seasoned with about 1 teaspoon salt. Pasta needs plenty of water, and plenty of space to expand while cooking, so use your largest pot. Bring water to a full, rolling boil over medium-high heat, add salt, add pasta, and cook according to the package directions. Pasta is best when cooked al dente, or "firm to the tooth." Drain pasta, and toss with sauce. Do not rinse pasta unless you'll be chilling it, as for pasta salad, because the added starch in cooked pasta helps bind it with the sauce.

Choose the right pot
Be sure you use a pot that's large enough to allow the pasta to move around while it boils. Overcrowding yields gummy results.

Al dente pasta
For perfect pasta, boil it only until it's al dente, or cooked but still slightly firm to the bite.

Cooking Dried Beans

When cooking dried beans and field peas, soak overnight in plenty of fresh water. Drain, rinse, and place in a heavy pot with 2 inches (5cm) water to cover. Bring to a boil over high heat, reduce heat to a simmer, add 1 teaspoon salt, and cook for about 1 hour or until tender.

If you're cooking kidney beans, you need to take an extra step. Raw kidney beans contain a toxin called phytohameaggluttinin, which can only be removed by cooking at the boiling point for 10 minutes. After bringing the beans and water to a boil, cook for 10 minutes, skimming off the foam that rises to the top. Then cook as directed. This step, while only 10 extra minutes, is essential.

Canned beans are easy and convenient, but dried beans are less expensive and their texture is incomparable when cooked from scratch. If you don't have time for an overnight soak, try the quick-soak method: bring beans to a boil in a large pot with 2 inches (5cm) water to cover. Boil for 10 minutes and then soak for 1 hour. Rinse, drain, and cook as directed. And don't throw away the bean broth—it's full of flavor and nutrients and perfect for use in soups and stews.

Storing cooked beans
You can refrigerate beans in their cooking liquid for up to 5 days or freeze for up to 3 months.

Cooking Lentils

Lentils do not require a soak and cook very quickly—as little as 20 minutes for red lentils and a little longer for other varieties. I like to cook lentils with a little onion and garlic to preseason them for recipes. In a medium saucepan over medium-high heat, heat 1 tablespoon olive oil. Chop a small onion and a few cloves of garlic, add them to the saucepan, and sauté for 3 to 5 minutes. Add 1 pound (450g) lentils with water or broth to cover by 2 inches (5cm). Bring to a boil, reduce heat to medium-low, and cook, partially covered, until tender. Divide into 2 cup portions plus cooking liquid, refrigerate for up to 5 days, or freeze for up to 3 months.

If you have issues digesting beans, soaking them removes most of the phytic acid and enzyme inhibitors that cause digestive distress. Add a strip of kombu to the cooking water to further increase the digestibility.

Perfect protein
Lentils are the perfect plant-based protein—nutritious, delicious, versatile, quick-cooking, and affordable.

Cooking with Tofu

Tofu is endlessly versatile. It's neutral in flavor so it takes on the flavor of whatever it's cooked with. Drain tofu before using it in recipes by placing the block on a cutting board that's wrapped in a clean kitchen towel. Set a heavy plate on top of tofu, and add a heavy can on top of that. Let tofu drain for 30 minutes, pat dry, and proceed with your recipe. Tofu can be sliced as for cutlets, cubed for stews and curries, crumbled for an eggless scramble, or blended into cake batters in place of eggs.

Tofu

Cooking with Tempeh

For best flavor and texture, marinate and/or steam tempeh. To steam, cut tempeh into strips or slices. Place it in a baking dish, cover with marinade or vegetable stock, cover tightly, and bake until tempeh is puffed up. This tenderizes and flavors your tempeh.

Cooking with Seitan

Seitan is a seasoned loaf made from vital wheat gluten that can be used to simulate the texture and flavors of beef or chicken. Try it grilled or seared in a cast-iron pan for use in sandwiches.

A quick trip to the produce aisle of a well-stocked grocery yields a variety of meat substitutes—hot dogs, sausages, veggie bacon, and pepperoni. The freezer section stocks "veggie crumbles" that can fill in for ground beef, veggie burgers, "chik'n" patties, and more. Try to limit your meat substitutes to homemade or store-bought seitan, tempeh, or tofu.

Hearty Seitan Roast
Brown and then bake loaves of Basic Seitan with sauces and vegetables for a hearty main dish with a meatlike texture.

Basic Seitan

You can find seitan in the refrigerated section of most grocery stores, or you can pick up some vital wheat gluten and make your own!

YiELD 2 (1-POUND/450G) LOAVES   **SERViNG** ⅙ LOAF   **PREP** 10 MiNS   **COOK** 30 MiNS

1   In a food processor fitted with a metal blade, blend 1½ cups vegetable stock; ½ small onion, roughly chopped; 1 garlic clove, roughly chopped; tamari; apple cider vinegar; Bell's seasoning; baking powder; and sweet paprika until smooth.

2   In a medium bowl, whisk together vital wheat gluten, chickpea flour, nutritional yeast, sea salt, and black pepper. Pour in wet ingredients, and stir with a silicone spatula until liquid is incorporated and a rough dough is formed.

3   Cut dough into 2 equal pieces, and use your hands to quickly knead into logs approximately 6 inches (15.25cm) long if the seitan will be served sliced, such as in roasts, cheese steaks, or gyros; or break seitan apart into rough chunks for stews or skewered items like satay. Set aside, and allow to rest for 5 minutes.

4   Meanwhile, chop remaining 1½ onions into rough wedges. Place in a large saucepan with a lid along with remaining 3½ cups vegetable stock, bay leaf, remaining 1 clove garlic, and porcini mushrooms (if using). Set over medium-high heat, bring to a boil, reduce heat to medium, and gently add seitan loaves. Cover and cook over the lowest heat for 45 minutes without lifting the lid.

5   Uncover, remove bay leaf, and cool completely in broth before storing. Seitan will keep in the refrigerator, stored in its cooking broth, for up to 3 days, or can be frozen for up to 3 months. Defrost completely in the refrigerator overnight before using.

INGREDIENTS

5 cups vegetable stock

2 small yellow onions

2 cloves garlic

1 TB. plus 1 tsp. reduced-sodium tamari

1 TB. apple cider vinegar

1 tsp. Bell's seasoning blend

1 tsp. baking powder

½ tsp. sweet paprika

1¾ cups vital wheat gluten

¼ cup chickpea flour

¼ cup nutritional yeast

½ tsp. fine sea salt

½ tsp. freshly ground black pepper

1 bay leaf

2 small pieces dried porcini mushroom (optional)

Seitan prepared in this manner can be marinated with any flavor you like. Grill or sear marinated seitan in a cast-iron frying pan for the best flavor.

Meal Plans

Here's a sample one-week meal plan, including many recipes from this book. Add a snack or two every day—such as nuts, seeds, and fresh fruit or vegetables dipped in a delicious dressing or spread like Tzatziki Sauce, Smoky Baba Ghanoush, or Romesco Sauce—and you're set.

When creating meal plans, think about your time, tastes, and the nutritional value of the foods you're eating. Also do as much cooking and prep work ahead of time as you can—a little work on your day off makes the rest of your week easier. Chop onions, celery, and carrots ahead; place in zipper-lock plastic freezer bags or containers in 1 cup portions; and use straight from the freezer—no need to thaw. Make a batch of granola on the weekend, and store it in an airtight jar for easy grab-and-go snacks. Soups and stews are ideal to make ahead and refrigerate or freeze for later. Prepare pizza dough up to 2 days ahead and refrigerate. Make a double recipe of Vinaigrette, refrigerate

Nutty Granola

	MONDAY	TUESDAY	WEDNESDAY
BREAKFAST	Nutty Granola* with fresh berries and plant-based yogurt	Breakfast Burritos, fresh melon with a squeeze of lime	Oatmeal, fresh blueberries
LUNCH	Roasted Beet Salad*, a hearty soup, 1 apple or pear	Herbed Tabbouleh*, Hummus*, whole-grain pita, 1 banana	Classic Vegetable Soup*, grilled cheese sandwich on whole-grain bread made with Pimiento Cheese* and sliced tomato, diced watermelon
DINNER	Stir-Fried Chinese Cress with Fermented Black Beans, Tom Yum Soup*, Seitan Satay*	Giambotta* over hot cooked polenta, green salad with Vinaigrette*, Sautéed Broccoli Rabe (blanch broccoli rabe in advance, add white beans for extra protein)	Oyster Mushroom Po'boys, Gumbo Filé*, green salad with Vinaigrette*

*Can be cooked in advance.

Roasted Beet Salad

for up to 5 days, shake, and pour over weekday salads. Whenever possible, double a soup or casserole recipe and freeze some in individual- or family-size portions. Soon you'll have a freezer full of meals ready to defrost whenever you're crunched for time.

THURSDAY	FRiDAY	SATURDAY	SUNDAY
Fruit-based breakfast smoothie, whole-grain English muffin with peanut butter and apple slices	Nutty Granola* with nondairy milk and sliced banana	Whole-Wheat Banana Pecan Pancakes, fresh berries	*Brunch:* Strawberry Muffins; Mushroom, Spinach, and Shallot Quiche*; Breakfast Sausage Patties
Sesame Noodles*, Sesame Asparagus*, sliced kiwi and strawberries	Pan Bagnat* (prep ingredients ahead, and assemble sandwiches in the morning), 1 apple or pear	Miso Udon Bowl*	Tofu Summer Rolls*, miso soup
Lentil and Vegetable Dal*, Naan, Sesame Tofu Cutlets	*Pissaladiere* (or homemade pizza; make dough and caramelized onions up to 2 days in advance), a hearty soup, green salad with Vinaigrette*	Tempeh Milanese*, Sautéed Mushroom Medley*, Summer Squash and Onion Bake*, freshly baked cookies	*Bisteeya*, Moroccan Couscous, Butternut Squash Tagine*, Chunky Applesauce

Grandma's Chicken-y Noodle Soup

Basics

Start with the simple things. Homemade ingredients such as stock, pastry dough, and nut milk are the building blocks of a perfect plant-based meal.

Caramelized Onions

When onions are cooked slowly in just a little bit of fat, their sugars caramelize, yielding a sweet, savory, dark brown mass of delicious flavor.

YIELD 1 CUP   **SERVING** ¼ CUP   **PREP** 5 MINS   **COOK** 45 MINS

1   Cut yellow onions in half, and peel. Trim root and blossom ends, and cut into ⅛-inch (3mm) slices.

2   In a 12-inch (30.5cm) sauté pan over medium-high heat, heat extra-virgin olive oil. Add onions, stir, and reduce heat to low. Stir in kosher salt and black pepper.

3   Cook, stirring every 10 minutes or so, for about 45 minutes or until onions are softened and dark golden brown. Onions should cook very slowly, browning gently and barely sizzling in the pan. Adjust heat as needed.

4   Use immediately, or refrigerate in a sealed container for up to 5 days.

INGREDIENTS

2 large yellow onions

1 TB. extra-virgin olive oil

¼ tsp. kosher salt

¼ tsp. freshly ground black pepper

Resist the urge to stir the onions frequently, or you'll fry them before their sugars are released. If you plan to double the recipe, use a larger pan. The onions must be in contact with the surface of the pan for caramelization to occur.

Simple Vegetable Stock (T)

This light and flavorful vegetable stock blends flavorfully well with other ingredients, making it the perfect base for any soup or sauce.

YIELD 4 QUARTS (4L) **SERVING** 1 or 2 CUPS **PREP** 15 MINS **COOK** 2 HOURS

1 In a large stockpot, combine leeks, yellow onions, carrots, celery, button mushrooms, bay leaf, Italian flat-leaf parsley, thyme, peppercorns, and tamari. Cover with filtered water.

2 Set over high heat, bring to a boil, cover, reduce heat to a gentle simmer, and cook for 2 hours.

3 Cool completely; strain and discard vegetables, herbs, and spices; and pour stock into glass jars or BPA-free containers for storage. Stock will keep in the refrigerator for up to 7 days or in the freezer for up to 3 months.

For *Golden Chicken-y Stock*, sauté leeks, carrots, and celery in 2 tablespoons extra-virgin olive oil for 10 minutes or until golden, and add 1 cup sliced cremini mushrooms and 1 healthy pinch saffron to the pot along with raw, unpeeled onions when you add water. For *Mushroom Stock*, follow the instructions for Golden Chicken-y Stock and increase cremini mushrooms to 2 cups. Cook vegetables in extra-virgin olive oil for 5 minutes longer (15 minutes total) to achieve a deeper level of caramelization, substitute 1 ounce (25g) dried porcini or forest mix mushrooms for saffron, and proceed as directed. For *Kombu Stock*, omit parsley, thyme, and bay leaf; replace all mushrooms with 2 cups sliced shiitake mushrooms and 1 ounce (25g) dried shiitake mushrooms; and add 2 (4-inch; 10cm) pieces of dried kombu to the pot.

INGREDIENTS

2 large leeks, halved lengthwise, washed, and cut into 1-in. (2.5cm) chunks

2 large yellow onions, root end trimmed and cut into 1-in. (2.5cm) chunks

4 medium carrots, scrubbed and cut into 1-in. (2.5cm) chunks

8 large stalks celery, cut into 1-in. (2.5cm) chunks

2 cups sliced button mushrooms

1 bay leaf

½ cup fresh Italian flat-leaf parsley leaves and stems

3 sprigs thyme

1 tsp. whole black peppercorns

2 TB. tamari or soy sauce

4 qt. (4L) filtered water

Pie Pastry (T)

This easy pie pastry comes together quickly in the food processor and yields a flaky, tender crust perfect for sweet or savory recipes.

YiELD 1 DOUBLE CRUST FOR A DEEP-DiSH PiE   **SERViNG** ABOUT ⅛ PiE   **PREP** 10 MiNS, PLUS 30 MiNS REST TiME   **COOK** NONE

1   In a food processor fitted with a metal blade, pulse all-purpose flour and kosher salt several times to combine.

2   Add half of shortening cubes, pulse 5 or 6 times, and run the food processor for 5 seconds. Add remaining shortening, and pulse until shortening resembles small, pea-size pieces.

3   Transfer flour mixture to a large bowl. Pour a few tablespoons ice water over flour mixture, and quickly toss with a large kitchen fork to combine. Continue adding water and tossing until mixture just comes together and then use the heel of your hand to press dough against the sides of the bowl to form a moist, cohesive ball.

4   Separate dough into two equal pieces, wrap in plastic wrap, and use your hands to flatten each piece into a 5-inch (12.5cm) disc.

5   Refrigerate dough for 30 minutes, and proceed as directed in your recipe.

INGREDiENTS

3 cups unbleached all-purpose flour

1½ tsp. kosher salt

12 TB. nonhydrogenated organic shortening, partially frozen, cut into small cubes

4 or 5 oz. (120 to 150ml) ice water

Removing the dough to a bowl before adding water ensures a tender crust. If you don't have a food processor, you can use a pastry blender to combine the flour, salt, and shortening.

Nut Milk (T)

Once you've tasted homemade nut milk, you'll never go back to the store-bought kind.

YiELD 4 CUPS   **SERViNG** 1 CUP   **PREP** 5 MiNS PLUS OVERNiGHT SOAK TiME   **COOK** NONE

1   Soak almonds in cold water overnight.

2   Discard water that the nuts soaked in, rinse nuts well, and drain.

3   In a high-speed blender, process nuts, filtered water, Medjool dates, vanilla extract, and cinnamon until smooth.

4   Using a nut milk bag, jelly bag, or clean stocking, strain solids from milk.

5   Refrigerate milk in a clean glass jar for up to 4 days. Shake well before using.

INGREDiENTS

1 cup raw almonds, hazelnuts, or cashews

4 cups filtered water

2 or 3 pitted Medjool dates

1 tsp. vanilla extract

½ tsp. ground cinnamon

For *Chocolate Nut Milk*, add ¼ cup raw cacao and 1 tablespoon agave nectar to the blender with other ingredients.

Fresh Pasta Dough

You can easily make your own eggless fresh pasta dough for long shapes such as hand-cut tagliatelle or fettuccine, or filled pasta such as ravioli. For added flavor and a pretty golden color, try saffron or tomato paste—or both. Use a pasta machine to roll the dough if you have one; a rolling pin also works. Try a straight pin without handles for this.

YIELD 1 POUND (450G) PASTA **SERVING** ¼ PASTA **PREP** 30 MINS **COOK** 3 MINS

1 In a small bowl, whisk extra-virgin olive oil into warm water. Whisk in tomato paste and/or saffron (if using).

2 In a large bowl, stir together all-purpose flour and kosher salt. Mound flour mixture on a wooden board or clean kitchen countertop, and make a well in the center. Pour olive oil–water mixture into the well.

3 Using a fork, slowly whisk flour mixture into olive oil mixture, a little at a time, until nearly all has been incorporated. Knead by hand for about 5 minutes, sprinkling your work surface with flour as you work. Add more water, a few drops at a time, if dough seems dry. When you've finished kneading, you should have a pliable ball of dough that's firm yet springy when pressed.

4 Wrap dough in plastic wrap, and rest at room temperature for 20 minutes. Meanwhile, prepare your pasta roller or dust your rolling pin and work surface with flour.

5 Using your fingers, press dough into a rectangle. Follow the instructions that came with your pasta machine, rolling dough until it's thin but not opaque. Or use a rolling pin to roll dough into a large rectangle, turning it a ¼ turn clockwise with each roll and flipping it over several times. Dust the board with flour frequently to prevent sticking.

6 Cut pasta into your desired shape, or fill, and cook in boiling, well-salted water for about 3 minutes or until tender. Serve immediately with your favorite sauce.

To make tagliatelle or other long pasta shapes, cut the rolled pasta dough into lengthwise thirds, and quickly roll up each piece from the short side, making a flat roll. Use a sharp knife to cut dough: ¼ inch (.5cm) for tagliatelle, ⅙ inch (1.5mm) for fettuccine, or ⅛ inch (3mm) for linguine. It's important to cut or fill pasta the moment it's been rolled, or it will dry out. Once you've mastered cut pasta, helpful tutorials for creating filled pasta shapes abound online. Experiment with different fillings: finely chopped and sautéed vegetables, puréed squash or beans, or nut cheeses such as Cashew Ricotta.

INGREDIENTS

2 TB. extra-virgin olive oil

1 cup warm water

1 tsp. tomato paste and/or 1 pinch saffron crushed in a mortar and pestle (optional)

3½ cups all-purpose flour, plus more for kneading

½ tsp. kosher salt

Sauces, Dressings, Dips, and Spreads

Dress a salad with style, top your plant-based creations with a satisfying sauce or gravy, or serve an array of delicious spreads and dips that will wow your dinner guests.

Hummus

Rich, creamy, nutritious hummus is redolent with the flavors of garlic, lemon, and tahini, a paste made of sesame seeds.

YIELD 4 OR 5 CUPS   **SERVING** ½ CUP   **PREP** 10 MINS PLUS OVERNIGHT SOAK TIME   **COOK** 1½ HOURS

1 Soak chickpeas in water overnight.

2 Discard soaking water, rinse chickpeas well, and drain.

3 In a large saucepan, place chickpeas. Add enough water to cover by 1 inch (2.5cm), and bring to a boil. Reduce heat to low so chickpeas bubble at a gentle simmer, and cook for 30 minutes.

4 Add kosher salt, and cook for 1 hour more or until chickpeas are soft and tender to the bite.

5 Drain chickpeas, reserving ¾ cup cooking liquid.

6 Place warm chickpeas in a food processor fitted with a metal blade. Add lemon juice, garlic, and tahini, and pulse to combine. With the machine running, slowly drizzle in ½ cup extra-virgin olive oil, followed by reserved cooking liquid.

7 Spread hummus in a shallow bowl, and make a well in the center. Pour remaining 2 tablespoons extra-virgin olive oil into the well, and sprinkle sumac over top to garnish. Serve immediately with warm pita bread, or refrigerate in a sealed container for up to 5 days.

INGREDIENTS

2 cups dried chickpeas

2 tsp. kosher salt

Juice of 1½ medium lemons (¼ cup)

2 cloves garlic, smashed and chopped

¼ cup tahini

½ cup plus 2 TB. extra-virgin olive oil

1 tsp. ground sumac

The secret to really great, creamy hummus is to use dried chickpeas and make the hummus while they're still warm. If you're in a hurry, you can make a passable hummus with canned chickpeas. For *Quick and Easy Hummus*, substitute 2 (14-ounce; 400g) cans chickpeas, rinsed and drained, for the cooked chickpeas in this recipe. Take the time to make it from scratch just once, though, and you might agree that sometimes the long way is the best way! If sumac is unavailable, search for online sources or substitute a squeeze of fresh lemon juice to imitate the tart, pucker-y, authentic flavor of ground sumac.

Smoky Baba Ghanoush ⓣ

The secret to excellent baba ghanoush is getting the eggplant charred on the outside, with the flesh on the inside collapsed upon itself. After the eggplant pulp is drained, it's mixed with tahini, garlic, lemon juice, and herbs for that signature creamy, smoky flavor no meze platter is complete without.

YIELD ABOUT 4 CUPS **SERVING** ½ CUP **PREP** 15 MINS **COOK** 30 MINS PLUS 1 HOUR DRAIN TIME

1 Preheat the oven to 450°F (230°C), or prepare a grill for direct, high heat.

2 Place eggplants directly on the oven or grill rack, and cook, turning once if grilling, for about 30 minutes or until skin is charred and flesh has begun to collapse into a soft mass. If cooking in the oven, place a baking sheet lined with aluminum foil on the rack below the eggplants to catch any drips.

3 Using a spatula, gently transfer eggplants to a cutting board, cut in half, remove seeds, and scoop flesh from charred skin into a fine-mesh sieve. Set over a large bowl, and drain for 1 hour. Discard liquid.

4 Place drained eggplant pulp in a food processor fitted with a metal blade. Add lemon juice, extra-virgin olive oil, tahini, garlic, and kosher salt, and process. You may choose to keep a chunky consistency by pulsing several times, or run the machine for 1 or 2 minutes for a smooth, creamy consistency.

5 Spoon baba ghanoush into a shallow bowl and serve immediately, or refrigerate in a sealed container for up to 5 days.

INGREDIENTS

2 large, firm eggplants

Juice of 1 to 1½ medium lemons (¼ cup)

¼ cup extra-virgin olive oil

3 TB. tahini

2 cloves garlic, smashed and chopped

1 tsp. kosher salt

It's important to take the time to thoroughly cook the eggplants. Undercooked eggplant is bitter and tough to chew. Thoroughly draining the eggplant flesh is another essential step. If you're in a hurry, gently press the flesh as it drains to facilitate removal of the bitter liquid. For a pretty and traditional garnish, sprinkle pomegranate seeds over the dish just before serving.

Tzatziki Sauce

Cool, creamy, plant-based yogurt combines with cucumber, garlic, and dill in this classic Greek sauce or dip. Try it with raw or grilled vegetables, or as a dip for warm pita.

YIELD ABOUT 2½ CUPS   SERVING ½ CUP   PREP 10 MINS PLUS 4 HOURS DRAIN AND CHILL TIME   COOK NONE

1   Place shredded cucumber in a fine-mesh sieve, sprinkle with kosher salt, toss, and set sieve over a bowl to drain for 30 minutes. Press cucumber gently, and discard liquid.

2   In a medium bowl, gently combine drained cucumber, yogurt, lemon juice, extra-virgin olive oil, dill, Italian flat-leaf parsley, and garlic.

3   Refrigerate for 3½ hours to chill and blend flavors before serving. Tzatziki will keep in the refrigerator for 3 days in a tightly sealed container.

INGREDIENTS

2 medium cucumbers, halved, seeded, and shredded

1 tsp. kosher salt

2 cups unflavored plant-based yogurt, such as coconut milk or soy

Juice of 1 medium lemon (3 TB.)

2 TB. extra-virgin olive oil

¼ cup fresh dill, finely chopped

2 TB. finely chopped fresh Italian flat-leaf parsley

2 cloves garlic, minced

Garlic

For *Extra Garlicky Tzatziki,* increase the garlic to 4 cloves. For *Fresh Mint Tzatziki,* add 2 tablespoons along with the dill and parsley.

Cashew Ricotta

Spread this nutty "cheese" on crackers, or use it as a filling for ravioli or lasagna. You'll love its light, airy texture of ricotta with a mild, cheesy flavor that's even better when heated.

YiELD 2 CUPS **SERViNG** ¼ CUP **PREP** 10 MiNS PLUS OVERNiGHT SOAK TiME **COOK** NONE

1 Soak cashews in water overnight.

2 Discard soaking water, rinse cashews well, and drain.

3 In a food processor fitted with a metal blade, process cashews, extra-virgin olive oil, warm water, lemon juice, nutritional yeast, parsley, chives, white (shiro) miso, marjoram, kosher salt, and black pepper until smooth, scraping down the bowl several times with a spatula.

4 Use immediately, or store in the refrigerator for up to 5 days.

iNGREDiENTS

2 cups raw cashews

¼ cup extra-virgin olive oil

¼ cup warm water

Juice of 1½ medium lemons (3 TB.)

2 TB. nutritional yeast

1 TB. finely chopped fresh parsley

1 TB. finely chopped chives

1 tsp. white (shiro) miso

½ tsp. dried marjoram

½ tsp. kosher salt

½ tsp. freshly ground black pepper

Pimento Cheese

Pimento cheese is a cheesy, addictive, piquant spread that's fabulous on sandwiches, with crackers, or stirred into cooked pasta for a fast and flavorful mac and cheese.

YiELD 3½ CUPS **SERViNG** ¼ CUP **PREP** 15 MiNS **COOK** NONE

1 In a food processor fitted with a metal blade, process cheddar-style cheese, cream cheese, mayonnaise, Vidalia onion, pimentos, garlic, hot sauce, sweet paprika, and cayenne until smooth.

2 Spoon pimento cheese into a serving bowl, and chill for 1 hour.

3 Serve immediately, or refrigerate for up to 3 days.

For a thicker spread perfect for *Grilled Cheese Sandwiches*, look for almond-based cheddar-style cheese, which is firmer than the tapioca-based products, and reduce the mayonnaise to ¼ cup. Spread sourdough or your favorite bread with a little plant-based butter on one side of each slice, and fill with a generous amount of Pimento Cheese. Heat a small sauté pan over medium heat, and toast your sandwich on both sides, turning once, until golden brown.

iNGREDiENTS

2 cups shredded plant-based cheddar-style cheese, preferably almond-based

8 oz. (225g) plant-based cream cheese

½ cup plant-based mayonnaise, such as Just Mayo

¼ large Vidalia onion, finely minced (¼ cup)

1 (4-oz.; 110g) jar pimentos, drained

1 clove garlic, finely chopped

½ tsp. Louisiana hot sauce, such as Crystal

½ tsp. sweet paprika

¼ tsp. cayenne

Nuts and Seeds

Many nuts and seeds are a good source of plant-based protein. Enjoy them as a snack, a main dish ingredient, or as butters and pastes. (Tahini, for example, is a paste made from sesame seeds.) And choose a wide variety for the most dietary value. Some nuts and seeds are better sources of protein, while others offer a wide array of vitamins and minerals.

Purchase raw or toasted, and once opened, store them in a tightly sealed glass jar. Store at room temperature for up to 1 month, or freeze for up to 6 months. Discard rancid nuts and seeds.

Almonds

	ALMONDS	BRAZIL NUTS	CASHEWS	CHESTNUTS	CHIA SEEDS	FLAXSEEDS	HAZELNUTS
USES	Soak for nut milks and cheeses. Use raw or toasted in sweet and savory recipes.	Use in salads, granola, pancakes, and baked goods.	Soak for nut milks and cheeses. Use raw or toasted in sweet and savory recipes.	Cut a X in the shell, and roast until chestnut opens. Use in desserts, sauté with vegetables, or purée for ravioli filling or in cookies.	Soak in warm water as an egg replacer. Sprinkle whole seeds on oatmeal, add to granola, or use in salads.	Grind and soak in warm water as an egg replacer. Add whole seeds or ground meal to pancakes, oatmeal, cookies, or desserts, or sprinkle on salads.	Soak for nut milks and cheeses. Toast and add to salads, such as pear and spinach. Use in baked goods, pesto, granola, and pasta dishes.
GOOD SOURCE OF ...	Protein, fiber, calcium, iron, riboflavin, manganese, magnesium, vitamin E, and potassium.	Protein, fiber, calcium, iron, magnesium, potassium, phosphorus, copper, and selenium.	Iron, magnesium, phosphorus, copper, manganese, and potassium.	Fiber, vitamin C, copper, and manganese.	Calcium, fiber, phosphorus, and manganese.	Protein, fiber, calcium, iron, magnesium, copper, phosphorus, thiamin, and manganese.	Protein, fiber, calcium, iron, vitamin C, vitamin E, copper, and manganese.

Brazil nuts

Flaxseeds

Pumpkin seeds

Macadamia nuts

Pistachios

Pecans

MACADAMIA NUTS	PECANS	PINE NUTS	PISTACHIOS	PUMPKIN SEEDS	SESAME SEEDS	SUNFLOWER SEEDS	WALNUTS
Use in baked goods, sprinkled on salads, or in granola or oatmeal.	Toast and add to baked goods, salads, oatmeal, granola, or sautéed vegetable dishes.	Toast and use for flavor and texture in pasta dishes, pesto, vegetable dishes, salads, and baked goods.	Add to pasta dishes, salads, dips, granola, and baked goods.	Toast and add to pesto, casseroles, pasta dishes, salads, dips, oatmeal, granola, and baked goods.	Use raw or toasted as a garnish for noodle dishes, stir-fries, and salads, or try in desserts. Use tahini (sesame paste) in dips and dressings.	Add to pesto, pasta dishes, sautéed vegetables, granola, or oatmeal.	Toast and use in desserts, pancakes, oatmeal, salads, pesto, and granola.
Protein, fiber, calcium, iron, thiamin, and manganese.	Protein, fiber, iron, calcium, and manganese.	Protein, iron, and manganese.	Protein, fiber, calcium, iron, vitamin B_6, copper, manganese, and potassium.	Protein, magnesium, zinc, and potassium.	Calcium, iron, magnesium, phosphorus, copper, manganese, and potassium.	Protein, iron, vitamins B_6 and E, magnesium, phosphorus, copper, manganese, selenium, and potassium.	Protein, calcium, iron, copper, and manganese.

Hazelnuts

Sesame seeds

Truffled Mushroom Pâté

This silky pâté with the umami flavors of mushrooms and truffles is an easy-to-make, elegant appetizer. Toss leftovers (if you have any) with hot, cooked pasta for a super-easy, creamy pasta dish.

YiELD 3 CUPS   SERVING ¼ CUP   PREP 15 MiNS   COOK 10 MiNS, PLUS SOAK AND CHiLL TiME

1 Soak cashews in cold water for at least 4 hours.

2 Discard water cashews soaked in, rinse nuts well, and set aside.

3 In a small bowl, place porcini mushrooms. Pour boiling water over top, and soak for about 5 minutes or until mushrooms are softened. Lift mushrooms from soaking water, agitating gently to release any soil. Reserve soaking liquid. Chop mushrooms, and set aside.

4 In a large sauté pan over medium-high heat, heat extra-virgin olive oil. Add shallots and garlic, and cook, stirring continuously, for 2 minutes.

5 Add porcini mushrooms, cremini mushrooms, white button mushrooms, and rosemary, and cook, stirring occasionally, for about 10 minutes or until mushrooms begin to brown, adjusting heat as necessary to keep mushrooms at a brisk sizzle without burning.

6 Deglaze the pan with white wine, and cook for 1 minute more. Season with kosher salt and black pepper, and remove from heat.

7 In a food processor fitted with a metal blade, combine cashews, mushroom mixture, white (shiro) miso, tamari, lemon juice, chives, and truffle oil.

8 Strain porcini liquid, leaving last 1 or 2 teaspoons to eliminate dirt. Pour into the food processor, and process until completely smooth. Taste pâté and season with additional kosher salt and black pepper if desired.

9 Pack pâté into a large ramekin or a terrine mold, and chill completely before serving with crackers or toasted French bread slices.

INGREDiENTS

1 cup raw cashews

½ oz. (25g) dried porcini mushrooms

½ cup boiling water

2 TB. extra-virgin olive oil

2 medium shallots, finely chopped (¼ cup)

2 cloves garlic, minced

1 (8-oz.; 225g) pkg. cremini (baby bella) mushrooms, sliced

1 (8-oz.; 225g) pkg. white button mushrooms, sliced

1 tsp. chopped fresh rosemary, or ½ tsp. dried

¼ cup dry white wine

½ tsp. kosher salt, or to taste

¼ tsp. freshly ground black pepper, or to taste

1 TB. white (shiro) miso

1 TB. reduced-sodium tamari

Juice of ½ medium lemon (1 TB.)

1 TB. finely chopped fresh chives

1 tsp. truffle oil, or to taste

Truffle oil has a very strong flavor. If you haven't had it before, you might want to begin with ½ teaspoon and add more to taste. For a milder truffle essence, omit the truffle oil and replace the kosher salt with truffle salt.

Béchamel Sauce

Smooth, creamy béchamel is the perfect choice when a cream sauce is desired. A hint of onion, clove, and nutmeg adds just a bit of spice to this delicious, versatile sauce.

YiELD 2 CUPS   **SERVING** ¼ CUP   **PREP** 5 MINS   **COOK** 10 TO 15 MINS

1 In a small saucepan over medium-high heat, heat grapeseed oil. Add all-purpose flour all at once, and stir vigorously with a whisk.

2 When flour mixture is golden and begins to smell nutty (but before it browns, about 2 minutes), add nondairy milk, continuing to whisk vigorously to prevent lumps.

3 Add clove-studded yellow onion and bay leaf, reduce heat to low, and cook, stirring frequently, for about 10 minutes or until sauce is thickened.

4 Remove from heat, and stir in kosher salt, black pepper, and nutmeg. Taste and adjust seasonings.

5 Strain sauce through a fine-mesh strainer to remove solids, and use immediately.

INGREDiENTS

¼ cup grapeseed oil

3 TB. all-purpose flour

2½ cups unflavored nondairy milk, preferably soy or rice

¼ small yellow onion, studded with 1 whole clove

1 bay leaf

¼ tsp. kosher salt

Pinch freshly ground black pepper

Pinch freshly grated nutmeg

Tomato Sauce

This simple, fresh-tasting tomato sauce comes together in minutes. Use the best-quality canned tomatoes you can find for this quick, easy sauce that's perfect with pasta or as a base for soup.

YiELD 3½ CUPS   **SERVING** ½ CUP   **PREP** 5 MINS   **COOK** 15 MINS

1 In a large saucepan over medium-high heat, heat extra-virgin olive oil. When oil is shimmering (but before it begins to smoke), add garlic and kosher salt. Cook, stirring, for 30 seconds, to allow garlic to release its fragrance without browning.

2 Add plum tomatoes with juice and white wine to the pan, and cook for 5 minutes.

3 Using a potato masher or a large fork, crush tomatoes. Reduce heat to medium, and cook, stirring occasionally, for 10 more minutes.

4 Stir in basil and black pepper, and remove from heat.

5 Use immediately, or pour into freezer-safe containers with 1-inch (2.5cm) headspace and freeze for up to 3 months.

INGREDiENTS

2 TB. extra-virgin olive oil

2 cloves garlic, peeled, smashed, and finely chopped

½ tsp. kosher salt

1 (28-oz.; 800g) can peeled plum tomatoes, with juice, preferably San Marzano

¼ cup dry white wine

4 leaves fresh basil, torn

¼ tsp. freshly ground black pepper

Mushroom Gravy

This rich, brown, flavorful gravy never disappoints. Using a well-flavored mushroom stock and taking time to cook the roux without burning it are the secrets to great gravy.

YiELD 4 CUPS   SERViNG ¼ CUP   PREP 10 MiNS   COOK 25 MiNS

1 In a medium sauté pan over medium-high heat, heat 3 tablespoons grapeseed oil until it shimmers (but before it begins to smoke). Add shallots, and cook, stirring occasionally, for about 5 minutes or until softened.

2 Add garlic, cremini mushrooms, and shiitake mushrooms, and cook, stirring often, for 10 minutes or until mushrooms have released their liquid.

3 Add Mushroom Stock and tamari, reduce heat to medium, and cook, stirring occasionally, while you make roux.

4 In a small saucepan over medium heat, heat remaining 2 tablespoons grapeseed oil. Whisk in all-purpose flour, and cook, stirring frequently, for about 10 minutes or until mixture is a rich brown color.

5 Whisk roux into mushroom mixture, and cook for about 5 to 10 more minutes or until gravy is as thick as you like it. Stir in bourbon (if using) and black pepper, and serve immediately. Gravy will keep in a tightly sealed container in the refrigerator for 3 days.

INGREDiENTS

5 TB. grapeseed oil

2 medium shallots, finely chopped (½ cup)

1 clove garlic, smashed and finely chopped

8 oz. (225g) cremini (baby bella) mushrooms, thinly sliced

8 oz. (225g) shiitake mushrooms, thinly sliced

4 cups *Mushroom Stock*

1 TB. low-sodium tamari or soy sauce

3 TB. all-purpose flour

1 TB. bourbon (optional)

½ tsp. freshly ground black pepper

Vinaigrette

Whisk together this simple, easily varied vinaigrette in minutes to give your salads and steamed veggies a flavorful punch.

YiELD 1 CUP   SERViNG 2 TABLESPOONS   PREP 10 MiNS   COOK NONE

1 In a small bowl, whisk together shallot, herbs, apple cider vinegar, kosher salt, and Dijon mustard.

2 Slowly whisk in extra-virgin olive oil, a few drops at a time, until dressing is smooth and all oil has been incorporated.

3 Whisk in black pepper, and use immediately, or refrigerate in a tightly sealed jar for up to 3 days.

Italian flat-leaf parsley

INGREDiENTS

1 medium shallot, finely minced (2 TB.)

2 TB. minced fresh herbs, such as chives, tarragon, or parsley

½ cup apple cider vinegar

½ tsp. kosher salt

1 TB. Dijon mustard

½ cup extra-virgin olive oil

½ tsp. freshly ground black pepper

UNREFINED OILS

You need some fat in your diet to keep your joints and skin healthy. Fat also provides flavor as well as that delicious, "fatty" mouthfeel to food, which makes some dishes more satisfying. Use minimally processed unrefined oils—such as extra-virgin olive oil; unrefined grapeseed or sunflower oil; and virgin, cold-pressed coconut oil—and in moderation. **Benefits** Lower cholesterol, control blood sugar levels, aid digestive health. **Uses** Opt for oil that hasn't been exposed to direct sunlight if you can, and use in dressings, for frying, and in baked goods. **Recipes** *Arancini,* Butternut Squash Tagine, *Imam Bayildi,* Summer Pesto, Vinaigrette.

Summer Pesto

Nothing evokes the flavor of warm summer days like fresh basil pesto. For the best flavor, make your pesto early in the season, when the basil is sweet and hasn't yet flowered.

YIELD 2 CUPS   **SERVING** ¼ CUP   **PREP** 15 MINS   **COOK** NONE

1   In a food processor fitted with a metal blade, pulse basil, pine nuts, almonds, nutritional yeast, and garlic until combined.

2   With the machine running, drizzle in lemon juice, followed by extra-virgin olive oil. Using a spatula, scrape down the sides of the bowl once or twice during this process.

3   Add kosher salt and black pepper, and pulse a few more times to combine.

4   Use immediately, or freeze for up to 6 months.

INGREDIENTS

2 cups tightly packed fresh basil leaves

½ cup pine nuts, toasted

2 TB. blanched sliced almonds, toasted

2 TB. nutritional yeast

1 clove garlic, smashed and chopped

Juice of 1 medium lemon (2 TB.)

½ cup extra-virgin olive oil

½ tsp. kosher salt

¼ tsp. freshly ground black pepper

Romesco Sauce

This savory Spanish sauce combines sweet roasted bell peppers, toasted almonds, bread fried in olive oil, and flavorful spices.

YIELD 1½ CUPS   **SERVING** ¼ CUP   **PREP** 25 MINS   **COOK** 5 MINS

1   In a small sauté pan over medium-high heat, heat 2 tablespoons extra-virgin olive oil for 1 minute or until it shimmers (but before it begins to smoke). Add bread, and fry, turning once, for 1 minute per side, or until golden on both sides.

2   In a food processor fitted with a metal blade, pulse bread, almonds, and garlic 5 or 6 times to combine.

3   Add plum tomatoes, red bell pepper, sherry vinegar, Italian flat-leaf parsley, crushed red pepper flakes, sweet paprika, kosher salt, and black pepper, and pulse several more times.

4   With the machine running, slowly drizzle in remaining 4 tablespoons extra-virgin olive oil, and process until well combined.

5   Use immediately, or refrigerate in a sealed container for up to 3 days.

INGREDIENTS

6 TB. extra-virgin olive oil

1 (1-in.; 2.5cm-thick) slice country bread, such as panella

½ cup sliced, blanched almonds, toasted and cooled

1 clove garlic, crushed and chopped

4 ripe plum tomatoes, cored and roughly chopped

1 red bell pepper, roasted, peeled, and cooled slightly

2 TB. sherry vinegar

1 TB. chopped fresh Italian flat-leaf parsley

1 tsp. crushed red pepper flakes

1 tsp. sweet paprika

½ tsp. kosher salt

¼ tsp. freshly ground black pepper

Pico de Gallo

Fresh salsa is easy to make, and it complements so many foods. Spoon it over tacos, breakfast sandwiches, or casseroles—or just enjoy it with crisp tortilla chips.

YIELD 2½ CUPS   SERVING ¼ CUP   PREP 15 MINS   COOK NONE

1   In a medium bowl filled with ice water, soak chopped red onion for 10 minutes.

2   Over an open gas flame using tongs, or under a broiler set to high, char poblano chile pepper on all sides. When skin is evenly charred, place poblano in a small bowl, cover with plastic wrap, and set aside for 2 minutes. Use a paper towel to rub skin off softened poblano, and core, seed, and finely chop poblano.

3   Core tomatoes, cut in half, and gently squeeze out seeds and pulp. Chop remaining flesh as finely as possible, and place in another medium bowl.

4   Drain onion in a colander, pat dry with a paper towel, and add to tomatoes. Stir in chopped poblano, cilantro, lime juice, and kosher salt.

5   Serve immediately, or refrigerate leftovers for up to 48 hours.

INGREDIENTS

½ small red onion, finely chopped (¼ cup)

1 poblano chile pepper

2 large tomatoes (to yield about 2 cups chopped)

¼ cup finely chopped fresh cilantro

Juice of 1½ medium limes (2 TB.)

½ tsp. kosher salt, or to taste

Guacamole

Creamy guacamole is a party essential, but it's not just for chips. Try it on sandwiches or salads or spooned onto enchiladas, nachos, and tacos. The key to an excellent guacamole is perfectly ripe Hass avocados. A ripe avocado has a dark skin, and the flesh yields when pressed gently.

YIELD 3 CUPS   SERVING ¼ CUP   PREP 10 MINS   COOK NONE

1   In a medium bowl, and using a fork, mash Hass avocado flesh to a chunky consistency.

2   Stir in lime juice, plum tomato, red onion, cilantro, jalapeño chile pepper, cumin, and kosher salt. Taste and add more kosher salt if necessary.

3   Serve immediately.

INGREDIENTS

4 ripe Hass avocados, pitted and peeled

Juice of 2 medium limes (4 TB.)

1 ripe plum tomato, cored, seeded, and finely chopped

½ small red onion, finely minced (¼ cup)

¼ cup finely chopped fresh cilantro

1 medium jalapeño chile pepper, seeded and finely minced

½ tsp. ground cumin

½ tsp. kosher salt, or to taste

Breakfasts

Give your body the nutrition it needs by starting with a healthy breakfast. Savor a leisurely weekend brunch, or dash out the door with a jar of granola.

Nutty Granola

Making your own granola is so easy, and you can add just what you want. Enjoy it as cold cereal with nondairy milk, layer it with yogurt and sliced fruit for a parfait, or just have some as an on-the-go snack.

YiELD 5 CUPS **SERViNG** ½ CUP **PREP** 5 MiNS **COOK** 20 TO 25 MiNS

1 Preheat the oven to 300°F (150°C).

2 In a large bowl, combine rolled oats, brown sugar, cinnamon, and kosher salt.

3 In a small bowl, whisk together grapeseed oil and maple syrup, and pour over oat mixture. Using a large spatula, fold ingredients together until everything is well mixed.

4 Spread granola on a large baking sheet, and bake for 20 to 25 minutes, stirring twice, until granola is toasted and golden brown.

5 Transfer to a clean bowl; stir in pecans, raisins, and pumpkin seeds; and allow to cool completely. Store in a tightly sealed glass jar for up to 1 week.

iNGREDiENTS

4 cups rolled oats (not instant)

2 TB. lightly packed brown sugar

1 tsp. ground cinnamon

½ tsp. kosher salt

½ cup grapeseed oil

½ cup maple syrup

½ cup chopped pecans, walnuts, or your favorite nut

½ cup raisins

¼ cup roasted, salted, shelled pumpkin seeds (pepitas)

You can easily customize this recipe. For *Nutty Chocolate Granola,* add some chocolate chips. For *Coconutty Granola,* add some flaked coconut. Change the nuts or seeds as you like, use as many different kinds of dried fruit as you like, include some candied ginger. Try cardamom or ground nutmeg instead of—or in addition to—the cinnamon.

Breakfast Burritos

For a fantastic on-the-go breakfast, cook some onions, mushrooms, and black beans with traditional sausage seasonings of sage and black pepper; load up on the toppings; roll; and go!

YIELD 2 BURRITOS   **SERVING** 1 BURRITO   **PREP** 10 MINS   **COOK** 10 MINS

1   In a medium sauté pan over medium-high heat, heat olive oil. Add red onion and button mushrooms, and cook for 2 or 3 minutes, stirring once or twice.

2   Add sage, kosher salt, and black pepper, and cook for 2 more minutes.

3   Stir in black beans, and cook, turning a few times and pressing to break up beans and brown them a little, for about 5 minutes. Remove from heat, and set aside.

4   Lay each tortilla on a plate, and spoon ½ of mushroom filling down center of each, and divide tomato, avocado, and salsa between each burrito. Roll burritos by folding the two short ends in first and then folding one long end inward.

INGREDIENTS

2 TB. olive oil

½ small red onion, thinly sliced (¼ cup)

2 cups sliced button mushrooms

1 tsp. crumbled dried sage

½ tsp. kosher salt

½ tsp. freshly ground black pepper

1 cup cooked black beans

2 (10-in.; 25cm) whole-wheat tortillas

1 large tomato, diced (1 cup)

1 medium Hass avocado, halved, seeded, and sliced

¼ cup prepared salsa

Button mushrooms

For a *Breakfast Scramble,* toss ½ cup crumbled silken tofu and 1 tablespoon nutritional yeast into the pan with black beans. Or add plant-based sour cream, chopped cilantro, or chopped fresh fruits or veggies to your burrito.

Whole-Wheat Banana Pecan Pancakes

Buckwheat flour, white whole-wheat flour, flax meal, and toasted pecans offer a boost of protein in the morning, with the sweet flavor of bananas and warm spices.

YiELD 12 PANCAKES   **SERViNG** 3 OR 4 PANCAKES   **PREP** 15 MiNS   **COOK** 10 MiNS

1   In a small saucepan over medium-high heat, warm ¼ cup soy milk.

2   Place flax meal in a small bowl, add warm milk, stir well, and set aside.

3   In a small bowl, whisk apple cider vinegar into remaining soy milk, and set aside to thicken and curdle.

4   In another small bowl, mash banana with brown sugar, maple syrup, and vanilla extract. Whisk in flax mixture, followed by curdled soy milk, and blend well.

5   Heat a cast-iron griddle or frying pan over medium heat until a drop of water sizzles and evaporates immediately.

6   Meanwhile, in a medium bowl, whisk together white whole-wheat flour, buckwheat flour, baking powder, kosher salt, cinnamon, and nutmeg. Stir in wet ingredients until just combined, and quickly fold in chopped pecans. Stir in more soy milk as needed to make a thick batter, the consistency of a heavy, pound cake batter.

7   Lightly oil or butter the griddle, and drop 3 tablespoon-size scoops of batter into the pan, spreading with a small spatula if necessary. Cook for 2 minutes without disturbing or until bubbles form on the surface of the pancakes, carefully flip over pancakes, and cook for 1½ more minutes. Grease the pan a little between each batch, as these pancakes will want to stick to the pan otherwise.

8   Serve hot with mixed fruit (if using) and more maple syrup (if using).

iNGREDiENTS

1¼ cups soy milk or coconut milk beverage, plus ¼ cup if needed

1 TB. flax meal (ground flaxseeds)

1 tsp. apple cider vinegar

1 large ripe banana, peeled and mashed well

1 TB. brown sugar

1 TB. maple syrup, plus more for serving (optional)

1 tsp. vanilla extract

1 cup white whole-wheat flour or whole-wheat pastry flour

⅓ cup buckwheat flour

2 tsp. baking powder

½ tsp. kosher salt

½ tsp. ground cinnamon

¼ tsp. ground nutmeg

½ cup finely chopped toasted pecans

1 cup fresh mixed raspberries, blueberries, and/or strawberries (optional)

The success of this recipe depends on using a nondairy milk that will curdle. Choose a soy or coconut milk beverage, as both will thicken and sour nicely when the apple cider vinegar is introduced.

Strawberry Muffins

These tender, biscuitlike muffins are kissed with a little bit of lemon and studded with bits of strawberry. For best results, skip the muffin liners and bake them directly in the tin.

YiELD 12 MUFFINS   **SERViNG** 1 MUFFIN   **PREP** 15 MiNS   **COOK** 22 TO 25 MiNS

1 Preheat the oven to 350°F (180°C). Lightly coat the cups of a 12-cup muffin tin with nonstick baking spray.

2 In a medium bowl, whisk together all-purpose flour, sugar, baking soda, baking powder, kosher salt, and nutmeg.

3 In a small bowl, whisk egg replacer with warm water until well blended. Whisk in vanilla nondairy yogurt, grapeseed oil, nondairy milk, lemon zest, and lemon juice.

4 Quickly stir wet ingredients into flour mixture until ingredients are just combined, taking care not to overmix. Fold in strawberries.

5 Using an ice-cream scoop or a large spoon, evenly divide batter among muffin cups. Batter will be thick, like biscuit dough.

6 Bake on the bottom rack of the oven for 22 to 25 minutes or until muffins spring back when lightly pressed in the center. Cool in the pan for 5 minutes before turning out on a wire rack to cool. Serve warm or at room temperature.

INGREDIENTS

1¾ cups all-purpose flour

½ cup sugar

½ tsp. baking soda

½ tsp. baking powder

¼ tsp. kosher salt

¼ tsp. ground nutmeg

3 tsp. egg replacer, such as Ener-G

¼ cup warm water

½ cup vanilla nondairy yogurt

¼ cup grapeseed oil

2 TB. nondairy milk

1 tsp. lemon zest

1 tsp. freshly squeezed lemon juice

1¼ cups roughly chopped fresh or frozen strawberries

For *Blueberry Muffins,* replace nutmeg with ¼ teaspoon ground cinnamon and strawberries with 1¼ cups fresh or frozen blueberries. If desired, combine 1 tablespoon raw sugar with ¼ teaspoon ground cinnamon, and sprinkle tops of muffins before baking.

Dairy Substitutes

Replacing dairy in your recipes is easy. A plethora of plant-based milks are available, such as soy, hemp, oat, almond, rice, and coconut. If you need a "milk" to curdle in a baking recipe, go with soy, hemp, or coconut. If you need the most neutral flavor possible, such as when making a sauce, rice milk is a good choice. When a rich, indulgent result is desired, try coconut milk coffee creamer. And don't overlook plant-based cheeses. There are some wonderful options out there.

Almonds

	ALMOND CHEESE	ALMOND MILK	CASHEW RICOTTA	COCONUT MILK BEVERAGE	COCONUT MILK COFFEE CREAMER	HEMP MILK
WHAT IT IS	Made from ground almonds or almond milk; it has a neutral, mozzarella-like flavor.	Made from ground almonds; it has a creamy texture and neutral, slightly sweet flavor.	Made from cashew milk; it has a creamy texture and nutty, savory flavor.	Made from grated coconut meat; it has a sweet, creamy taste.	Made with coconut milk, sweeteners (such as maple syrup or stevia), and flavorings (such as vanilla); it's sweet and creamy.	Made from a blend of ground hemp seeds and water; it has a nutty, fairly neutral flavor.
USES	Melting and in cheese sauces, sandwiches, lasagna, and pasta dishes.	Drinking, cooking, and baking.	Hors d'oeuvres and lasagna.	Drinking, cooking, and baking (curdles when acid is added).	Rich and creamy desserts. Use in desserts when a creamy consistency is needed.	Drinking, cooking, and baking (curdles when acid is added).
GOOD SOURCE OF ...	Protein and calcium.	Vitamins A and D and calcium. (See label for fortified products.)	Iron, magnesium, phosphorus, copper, manganese, and potassium.	Vitamins A and B_{12} and calcium.	High in calories and low in nutrients—use sparingly.	Protein and iron. (See label for fortified products.)

Cashews

Coconut

Brazil nuts

Rice

Soybeans

NUT MiLK	OAT MiLK	RiCE MiLK	SOY MiLK	TAPiOCA CHEESE
Made from ground nuts, such as Brazil nuts, hazelnuts, pecans, or macadamias; flavor varies by the nut used.	Made with oats, water, and flavorings; it has a slightly sweet and nutty flavor.	Made from unsweetened brown rice; it has a neutral flavor and works well in savory recipes.	Made from ground dried soybeans and water; it has a slightly sweet flavor and is also available in vanilla and chocolate flavors.	A mozzarella-style cheese made from cassava root starch; it has a tangy flavor and melts well.
Drinking, cooking, and baking.	Drinking, cooking, and baking.	Drinking and cooking when a neutral flavor is desired.	Drinking, cooking, and baking (curdles when acid is added).	Melting and in cheese sauces and sandwiches.
Varies by nut.	Protein, iron, fiber, phosphorus, and selenium. (See label for fortified products.)	Not a significant source of nutrients unless fortified—use sparingly. (See label for fortified products.)	Protein, iron, magnesium, and selenium. (See label for fortified products.)	Not a significant source of nutrients—use sparingly. (See label for fortified products.)

Hazelnuts

Oats

Mushroom, Spinach, and Shallot Quiche

Using chickpea flour instead of tofu gives this quiche a smooth texture and pleasant flavor that makes an excellent base for traditional quiche ingredients. This version is chock full of sweet, lightly caramelized shallots; sautéed mushrooms; and spinach.

YiELD 1 (9-INCH; 23CM) QUICHE **SERVING** ⅛ QUICHE **PREP** 15 MINS **COOK** 60 MINS

1 Preheat the oven to 350°F (180°C).

2 Roll out Pie Pastry to an 11-inch (28cm) circle, and transfer to a 9-inch (23cm) deep-dish pie pan. Fold edges of dough inward, and crimp using your thumb and two fingers to pinch dough all around. Refrigerate until ready to fill.

3 In a large sauté pan over medium heat, heat 2 tablespoons extra-virgin olive oil. Add shallots, and cook, stirring once, for 4 minutes or until they begin to brown.

4 Add button mushrooms, and cook, stirring frequently, for about 5 minutes or until mushrooms are golden.

5 Add spinach, ½ teaspoon kosher salt, and black pepper, and stir until wilted. Set aside.

6 In a medium saucepan over medium heat, bring water and vegetable stock to a boil.

7 In a small bowl, whisk together chickpea flour, nutritional yeast, turmeric, and sweet paprika.

8 Add remaining 2 tablespoons extra-virgin olive oil to boiling stock mixture, and pour in chickpea flour a little at a time, whisking vigorously to eliminate lumps. Continue whisking for 2 minutes or until mixture thickens, and whisk in remaining ½ teaspoon kosher salt, plant-based butter, and chives. Stir in mushroom mixture.

9 Pour cooked mixture into the prepared piecrust, and bake for 40 minutes or until filling is set. Cool for 20 minutes before slicing. Serve warm or cold.

INGREDIENTS

1 batch *Pie Pastry* for a 9-in. (23cm), single-crust, deep-dish pie

4 TB. extra-virgin olive oil

4 shallots, thinly sliced (1 cup)

6 oz. (170g) white button mushrooms, thinly sliced

1 (5-oz.; 140g) pkg. baby spinach

1 tsp. kosher salt

¼ tsp. freshly ground black pepper

1½ cups water

1 cup vegetable stock

1 cup chickpea flour

2 TB. nutritional yeast

½ tsp. turmeric

Pinch sweet paprika

1 TB. plant-based butter

2 TB. finely chopped fresh chives

For a *"Cheesy" Breakfast Quiche*, add ½ cup of your favorite shredded plant-based cheese.

Breakfast Sausage Patties

Salty, tasty, and perfectly spiced, this plant-based sausage is packed with protein. Make a big batch and freeze them for rushed weekday mornings.

YiELD 2 (3-INCH; 7.5CM) PATTIES   **SERVING** 1 PATTY   **PREP** 10 MINS   **COOK** 4 MINS

1 In a small bowl, whisk together flax meal and warm water. Set aside.

2 In a medium sauté pan over medium-high heat, heat 1 tablespoon grapeseed oil. Add yellow onion and cremini mushrooms, and cook, stirring frequently, for 10 minutes or until onions soften and mushrooms begin to brown.

3 Stir in sage, thyme, marjoram, nutmeg, and cloves, and stir for 1 minute. Season with kosher salt and black pepper, and set aside to cool slightly.

4 In a food processor fitted with a metal blade, pulse black beans, dark kidney beans, quinoa, rolled oats, gluten-free all-purpose flour, mushroom mixture, and flax mixture 5 or 6 times or until mixture reaches a chunky but cohesive consistency.

5 Heat a large nonstick frying pan over medium heat, add just enough grapeseed oil to coat the bottom of the pan (about 2 or 3 tablespoons). Using an ice-cream scoop, scoop out scant ¼ cup portions of bean mixture directly into the hot pan, spacing them several inches apart. Use the back of a wet tablespoon to gently pat each down into a 3-inch (7.5cm) patty. Cook for 2 minutes per side, turning carefully with a thin spatula (patties are somewhat delicate). Serve immediately, or cool completely and freeze in an airtight container separated by layers of parchment paper. Reheat frozen sausage patties in the microwave for about 1 minute or in a 400°F (200°C) oven for 8 to 10 minutes.

INGREDIENTS

1 TB. flax meal (ground flaxseeds)

3 TB. warm water

1 TB. grapeseed oil, plus more for frying

1 small yellow onion, finely chopped (about ½ cup)

6 oz. (170g) cremini (baby bella) mushrooms, finely chopped

2 tsp. crumbled dried sage

1½ tsp. dried thyme

1 tsp. dried marjoram

½ tsp. ground nutmeg

Pinch ground cloves

2 tsp. kosher salt

1 tsp. freshly ground black pepper

1 (14-oz.; 400g) can black beans, rinsed and drained

1 (14-oz.; 400g) can dark kidney beans, rinsed and drained

1 cup cooked quinoa

2 TB. rolled oats

1 TB. gluten-free all-purpose flour or fine cornmeal

For *Spicy Sausage Patties,* sauté 1 finely minced jalapeño chile pepper along with onions and mushrooms.

AVOCADOS

This tropical fruit is a favorite in Mexican dishes. It has a smooth texture; a nutty flavor; packs a nutritional wallop; and pairs well with tomatoes, grapefruit, limes, mangoes, pineapple, sugar, and balsamic vinegar. **Benefits** High in fiber and potassium, lowers blood pressure, is anti-inflammatory, lubricates joints. **Uses** Opt for firm avocados and let them ripen at home, or choose ripe ones by pressing gently on the shoulder area and feeling for "give." Eat fresh in salads, in soups, or spread on whole-grain toast and topped with a Breakfast Sausage Patty and sliced tomato for a quick breakfast sandwich. **Recipes** Guacamole, Breakfast Burritos, *Posole.*

Sandwiches, Burgers, and Wraps

You'll find a world of flavors in these tasty meat-free recipes, from classic muffuletta, to authentic po'boys, to Asian-inspired sandwiches with delicious sauces. Enjoy as lunch or with soup for supper.

Bánh Mì Portobello Burgers (T)

The humble portobello mushroom makes a delicious, all-natural substitute for hamburger patties. This savory take on a traditional Vietnamese sandwich is packed with flavor: a meaty-tasting mushroom "burger," crunchy pickled veggies, and spicy Sriracha "mayo" are piled on a crusty baguette.

YiELD 4 SANDWICHES   **SERVING** 1 SANDWICH   **PREP** 40 MINS   **COOK** 10 MINS

1 In a small bowl, whisk together lime juice, tamari, toasted sesame oil, garlic powder, and ginger.

2 Wipe each portobello mushroom clean with a damp paper towel, place mushrooms in a zipper-lock plastic bag, pour in lime juice marinade, seal the bag, and shake gently to distribute marinade. Set aside.

3 In a medium bowl, gently toss daikon radish and carrot.

4 In a small saucepan over medium heat, combine rice vinegar, water, sugar, and kosher salt. Bring to a boil, stirring to dissolve sugar and salt.

5 Pour vinegar mixture over daikon and carrot, stir, and set aside for about 30 minutes.

6 In another small bowl, whisk together plant-based mayonnaise and Sriracha hot sauce.

7 Heat a grill to direct, high heat, or set a grill pan over high heat on your stovetop. Place mushrooms on the grill, gill side down, and cook for 3 minutes. Turn over mushrooms, and cook for 2 more minutes or until mushrooms are juicy and tender.

8 During the last minute of mushroom cook time, place baguette rolls on the grill, split side down, and toast.

9 Drain pickled vegetables in a fine-mesh strainer.

10 To assemble sandwiches, spread ¼ mayonnaise mixture on one side of each roll, and add a layer of English cucumber slices. Place 1 portobello burger on each sandwich, and top with ¼ drained pickled vegetables. Garnish with cilantro leaves (if using), and serve immediately.

INGREDIENTS

Juice of 1 medium lime (2 TB.)

2 TB. reduced-sodium tamari or soy sauce

1 tsp. toasted sesame oil

½ tsp. garlic powder

½ tsp. ground ginger

4 large portobello mushrooms, stems removed

1 small daikon radish, peeled and shredded (1 cup)

1 medium carrot, shredded (½ cup)

¼ cup rice vinegar

¼ cup water

1 TB. sugar

1 tsp. kosher salt

2 TB. plant-based mayonnaise, such as Vegenaise

1 tsp. Sriracha hot sauce

4 (4-in.; 10cm) crusty baguette rolls, split

½ English cucumber, thinly sliced

Cilantro leaves (optional)

Daikon radish, also known as Japanese horseradish, is a staple in Asian cuisine. It resembles a large, white parsnip and has a mild, radishlike flavor. Smaller varieties are terrific raw or lightly pickled, while the larger roots can be thinly sliced and baked as chips or shredded and pan-fried for a unique alternative to a potato pancake.

Italian Eggplant Cutlet Subs

Crispy breading surrounds tender eggplant slices in these subs, layered on a hearty roll with sliced hot peppers, lettuce, tomato, shaved onion, and plenty of olive oil and red wine vinegar.

YiELD 4 SANDWICHES **SERViNG** 1 SANDWiCH **PREP** 15 MiNS **COOK** 15 MiNS

1 Sprinkle kosher salt over eggplant slices, place eggplant in a colander, and set aside to drain for 10 minutes. Pat slices dry, squeezing gently to remove any bitter liquid.

2 In separate shallow bowls, place water, all-purpose flour, and Italian-seasoned breadcrumbs.

3 Bread eggplant slices in the following manner: dip each slice in water, then in flour, quickly dip in water again, followed by breadcrumbs. Dredge one last time in flour, and shake off any excess. Set aside each breaded slice, and continue until all slices are breaded.

4 In a large fry pan over medium-high heat, heat enough olive oil (or grapeseed oil) to come ¼ inch (.5cm) up the side of the pan for shallow frying. When oil shimmers, add eggplant slices a few at a time, taking care not to crowd the pan. Fry for about 2 minutes or until golden and crispy, turn over slices, and fry the other side until golden. Set cooked slices aside on a paper towel–lined baking sheet, and repeat until all eggplant has been fried.

5 Heat a broiler to high, place split Italian rolls on a baking sheet, and toast for 2 or 3 minutes or until golden. Rub toasted rolls with cut garlic clove, and drizzle rolls evenly with 2 tablespoons olive oil.

6 To assemble sandwiches, evenly divide eggplant slices among rolls. Top with tomato, romaine lettuce, and red onion slices, again evenly distributing ingredients. Place a few hot cherry pepper slices (if using) on each sandwich, drizzle with red wine vinegar, and serve.

INGREDiENTS

½ **tsp.** kosher salt

1 large Italian eggplant, sliced lengthwise in ¼-inch (.5cm) slices

½ **cup** water

½ **cup** all-purpose flour

½ **cup** Italian-seasoned breadcrumbs

4 (6-in.; 15.25cm) Italian rolls, sliced horizontally

1 clove garlic, halved

2 TB. olive oil, plus more for frying

2 medium tomatoes, sliced

2 cups shredded romaine or iceberg lettuce

½ small red onion, sliced paper thin

Sliced hot cherry peppers in oil, drained (optional)

2 TB. red wine vinegar

For *Eggplant Parm Subs*, fry eggplant slices and toast rolls as directed. Spoon ½ cup Tomato Sauce over each sandwich, top each with ¼ cup of your favorite shredded plant-based mozzarella cheese, and broil until melted.

Oyster Mushroom Po'boys

Oyster mushrooms are breaded in cornmeal, quickly fried until crisp, and slathered with a savory dressing and shredded lettuce on soft rolls. Delicious!

YIELD 4 SANDWICHES **SERVING** 1 SANDWICH **PREP** 15 MINS **COOK** 5 MINS

1 In a small bowl, combine mayonnaise, ketchup, grated onion, sweet pickle relish, and chives. Refrigerate until ready to use (can be made up to 3 days in advance).

2 In a large fry pan over medium heat, heat enough grapeseed oil to come ¾ inch (2cm) up the sides of the pan.

3 In separate shallow bowls, place water, all-purpose flour, and cornmeal.

4 Bread oyster mushrooms as follows: dip each in water, then in flour, quickly dip in water again, and then dredge thoroughly in cornmeal. Set aside each mushroom, and continue until all mushrooms are breaded.

5 Add breaded mushrooms to the fry pan, and fry for about 3 minutes, turning once or twice, until golden on all sides. Drain on paper towels, and sprinkle with Old Bay seasoning and sweet paprika.

6 Pile mushrooms generously onto sub rolls, drizzle each sandwich with about 1 tablespoon dressing, top with iceberg lettuce, and serve with lemon wedges on the side.

INGREDIENTS

¼ **cup** plant-based mayonnaise

1 TB. ketchup

1 TB. grated fresh sweet onion

1 TB. sweet pickle relish

1 tsp. finely chopped chives

Grapeseed oil

½ **cup** water

1 cup all-purpose flour

1 cup fine cornmeal

¾ **lb. (340g)** oyster mushrooms, pulled apart into "oyster-size" chunks

1 tsp. Old Bay seasoning

½ **tsp.** sweet paprika

4 (6-in.; 15.25cm) soft "sub" rolls, sliced horizontally

2 cups shredded iceberg lettuce

Lemon wedges

Oyster mushrooms

Muffuletta (T) (UNDER 30)

Muffuletta is a classic New Orleans sandwich that features a whole round loaf of crusty bread, hollowed out and slathered in a salty, savory olive salad of the same name. Grilled vegetables are a healthy and delicious alternative to the fatty meats that usually fill this sandwich. This recipe is a great choice for picnics because you can pack a well-wrapped muffuletta, allow the flavors to marry, and slice it just before serving.

YIELD 1 (10-INCH; 20CM) ROUND SANDWICH　**SERVING** ¼ SANDWICH　**PREP** 20 MINS　**COOK** 15 MINS

1　In a medium bowl, combine green olives, oil-cured black olives, giardiniera, capers, celery, carrot, garlic, oregano, and 2 tablespoons extra-virgin olive oil. Stir in crushed red pepper flakes, and set aside.

2　Preheat a grill pan or a grill for direct, high heat.

3　In a large dish, stir together 1 tablespoon extra-virgin olive oil and balsamic vinegar. Add portobello mushrooms and zucchini, and toss gently to coat. Sprinkle with kosher salt and black pepper. Transfer vegetables to the grill pan or grill, and cook for 2 minutes per side. Set aside.

4　Cut bread in half horizontally, and use your hands to pull out most of soft insides of bread. (Save it to make breadcrumbs!)

5　Layer grilled mushrooms and zucchini evenly over bread, followed by olive salad. Top with baby arugula and red onion, and drizzle with remaining 1 tablespoon olive oil and red wine vinegar. Press sandwich gently to pack layers tightly. Cut sandwich into quarters and serve, or wrap tightly in plastic wrap for up to 4 hours.

INGREDIENTS

¾ cup pimiento-stuffed green olives, roughly chopped

½ cup pitted oil-cured black olives, roughly chopped

½ cup giardiniera mix, such as Victoria, roughly chopped

2 TB. salt-packed capers, rinsed and drained

2 TB. finely chopped celery

2 TB. finely chopped carrot

2 cloves garlic, finely chopped

1 tsp. dried oregano

4 TB. extra-virgin olive oil

Pinch crushed red pepper flakes

2 TB. balsamic vinegar

3 portobello mushrooms, cut in ¼-in.-thick (.5cm-thick) slices

1 large zucchini, sliced lengthwise in ¼-in.-thick (.5cm-thick) slices

½ tsp. kosher salt

½ tsp. freshly ground black pepper

1 (10-in.; 20cm) round loaf country bread, preferably semolina

2 cups baby arugula

½ small red onion, sliced paper thin

2 TB. red wine vinegar

Giardiniera is a delicious mix of pickled vegetables that usually includes cauliflower, carrot, celery, and pepperoncini (pickled peppers) preserved in vinegar. You can find it in grocery stores or Italian delis.

Falafel Burgers

These pita sandwiches pack all the deliciously spiced flavor of traditional falafel without the deep-fried fat.

YIELD 8 BURGERS/4 SANDWICHES SERVING 2 BURGERS/1 SANDWICH PREP 15 MINS COOK 10 MINS

1. In a small bowl, combine flax meal and 3 tablespoons warm water. Set aside.

2. In a small sauté pan over medium heat, heat 2 tablespoons extra-virgin olive oil until it shimmers (but before it begins to smoke). Add yellow onion, cumin, and coriander, and sauté, stirring constantly, for 5 minutes or until onion softens and begins to brown.

3. Stir in kosher salt, black pepper, lemon zest, and 2 tablespoons lemon juice. Remove from heat, and stir in cilantro and Italian flat-leaf parsley.

4. In a food processor fitted with a metal blade, process chickpeas, breadcrumbs, and onion mixture for 1 minute or until chunky. Reserve ¼ cup mixture. Continue to process, adding flax mixture, remaining 2 tablespoons extra-virgin olive oil, and reserved liquid from chickpeas, until smooth. Pulse in reserved chickpea mixture in one or two pulses, just to evenly distribute. Divide mixture into 8 evenly sized burgers 3 inches (7.5cm) wide and about 1 inch (2.5cm) thick.

5. In a large nonstick sauté pan over medium-high heat, heat grapeseed oil. Add falafel burgers, and cook, turning once, until both sides are golden brown and falafel burgers are heated through.

6. In a small bowl, whisk together tahini, garlic, and remaining 2 tablespoons lemon juice. Add 1 or 2 tablespoons warm water or enough to make a smooth dressing.

7. Fill each pita with 2 falafel burgers and evenly divide plum tomatoes, romaine lettuce, and red onion among pitas. Drizzle each pita with ¼ tahini mixture, and serve immediately.

For *Gluten-Free Falafel*, use fresh gluten-free breadcrumbs, and serve burgers over a green salad.

INGREDIENTS

1 TB. flax meal (ground flaxseeds)

4 or 5 TB. warm water

4 TB. extra-virgin olive oil

1 medium yellow onion, finely chopped (about ½ cup)

2 tsp. ground cumin

1 tsp. ground coriander

½ tsp. kosher salt

¼ tsp. freshly ground black pepper

1 tsp. lemon zest

Juice of 2 medium lemons (4 TB.)

¼ cup finely chopped fresh cilantro

2 TB. finely chopped fresh Italian flat-leaf parsley

2 (14-oz.; 400g) cans chickpeas, drained and rinsed (or 3 cups cooked chickpeas), ¼ cup liquid reserved

1 cup fresh breadcrumbs (from 1 or 2 slices bread)

3 TB. grapeseed oil

2 TB. tahini

1 clove garlic, minced

4 small loaves pita bread, split on one side

2 medium plum tomatoes, finely diced (½ cup)

½ cup thinly sliced romaine lettuce

½ medium red onion, thinly sliced

Pan Bagnat (T) (UNDER 30)

Chickpeas and artichoke hearts are seasoned with dulse, a seaweed flake, along with capers and vinegar, for a delicious new take on this Niçoise "street food" classic. The resulting chickpea spread also makes an excellent spread for crostini!

YIELD 4 SANDWICHES SERVING 1 SANDWICH PREP 20 MINS COOK NONE

1 In a food processor fitted with a metal blade, pulse chickpeas, artichoke hearts, reserved artichoke heart marinade, capers, red wine vinegar, and dulse flakes until a rough, chunky purée consistency is reached.

2 Divide chickpea mixture equally among whole-wheat rolls. Top with tomato slices, romaine lettuce, and red onion slices.

3 Sprinkle Niçoise olives over vegetables, drizzle each sandwich with 1 tablespoon extra-virgin olive oil, and season liberally with black pepper. Serve with plenty of napkins!

INGREDIENTS

1 (14-oz.; 400g) can chickpeas, rinsed and drained

1 (6-oz.; 170g) jar marinated grilled artichoke hearts, drained, 2 TB. marinade reserved

1 TB. salted capers, rinsed and drained

1 TB. red wine vinegar

1 tsp. dulse flakes

4 crusty round whole-wheat rolls, sliced

2 large tomatoes, sliced

4 leaves romaine lettuce

½ small red onion, sliced paper thin

2 TB. chopped, pitted Niçoise olives

¼ cup extra-virgin olive oil

½ tsp. freshly ground black pepper

Capers

Pan bagnat means "bathed bread," which alludes to the generous amounts of olive oil slathered on this delicious sandwich. You'll need a roll that can stand up to this kind of treatment, so look for the sturdiest country bread you can find. Pan bagnat is traditionally sold in individual paper-wrapped portions, but you can pack all the fillings into a large, round loaf in the manner of muffuletta to serve a crowd. If you have extra time, add lightly steamed haricot verts (French green beans) to this sandwich for extra nutrition and crunch.

Korean Barbecue Sliders

These little sandwiches pack a lot of flavor. Tempeh is steamed, smothered in a savory Korean barbecue sauce, piled on slider buns, and topped with a crunchy salad. The prep time seems long, but most of it is spent chopping ingredients and steaming and marinating the tempeh.

YIELD 8 SLIDERS **SERVING** 2 OR 3 SLIDERS **PREP** 45 MINS **COOK** 10 MINS

1. Place tempeh in a small sauté pan, cover with water, set over medium heat, and bring to a simmer. Cover and cook for 10 minutes. Remove lid, drain, and cool.

2. Cut tempeh into 2 horizontal slices, and cut each of those into 4 equal pieces, so you have 8 small "burgers." Place tempeh slices in a shallow pan that will accommodate them in a single layer.

3. In a small saucepan over high heat, combine ½ cup tamari, brown sugar, garlic, sambal oelek, ginger, 1 tablespoon rice vinegar, and 1 teaspoon sesame oil. Bring to a boil.

4. In a small bowl, combine cornstarch and cold water until smooth. Add to sauce in the saucepan, and cook for about 1 minute or until thickened.

5. Pour hot barbecue sauce over tempeh, and marinate at room temperature for 30 minutes (or for up to 24 hours in the refrigerator).

6. Preheat a broiler to high.

7. In a medium bowl, whisk together remaining 2 teaspoons rice vinegar, remaining 1 teaspoon tamari, remaining 1 teaspoon sesame oil, toasted sesame seeds, and granulated sugar. Set aside.

8. Broil tempeh slices, turning once, until hot and crispy. Place 1 tempeh slice on each bun.

9. In a small bowl, toss romaine lettuce and radishes with dressing. Distribute equally among sandwiches, and serve immediately.

INGREDIENTS

1 (8-oz.; 225g) pkg. tempeh

½ cup plus 1 tsp. reduced-sodium tamari

½ cup brown sugar, firmly packed

3 cloves garlic, finely chopped

1 TB. sambal oelek (chili garlic sauce)

1 TB. finely chopped fresh ginger

1 TB. plus 2 tsp. rice vinegar

2 tsp. toasted sesame oil

1 TB. cornstarch

1 TB. cold water

1 tsp. toasted sesame seeds

1 tsp. granulated sugar

8 small buns, such as whole-wheat dinner rolls or slider buns

1 cup shredded romaine lettuce

½ cup thinly sliced radishes

Instead of using water to cook the tempeh, you could substitute vegetable stock. Also, check the ingredients on your rolls. I like to get mine from a local bakery, which ensures that they're minimally processed and completely plant based.

Soups and Stews

Soups and stews are the perfect transition food: healthy, hearty, and satisfying. You won't mind eating your vegetables when you're enjoying a big bowl of deeply flavored, satisfying comfort.

Grandma's Chicken-y Noodle Soup

This soup is just the thing if you or someone you love is feeling under the weather. A gently seasoned, golden broth is accented with fresh vegetables, herbs, and pasta for a perfect bowl of comfort.

YIELD 5 CUPS   SERVING 1 CUP   PREP 10 MINS   COOK 20 MINS

1   Bring a medium pot of salted water to a boil over high heat, add spaghetti, and cook according to the package directions until pasta is al dente (cooked but firm to the bite). Drain, rinse with cold water, and set aside.

2   In a large saucepan over medium-high heat, heat extra-virgin olive oil. Add onion, reduce heat to medium, and cook, stirring frequently, for 5 to 10 minutes or until onion is golden and softened.

3   Add carrot, celery, parsnip, garlic, and kosher salt, and cook for 3 minutes.

4   Stir in Golden Chicken-y Stock, nutritional yeast, tamari, and black pepper. Increase heat to high, bring to a boil, reduce heat to medium, and simmer for 10 minutes.

5   Stir in spaghetti, and cook for 1 more minute.

6   Stir in Italian flat-leaf parsley and dill, and serve immediately.

INGREDIENTS

2 oz. (55g) spaghetti or fettuccine, broken into small pieces

1 TB. extra-virgin olive oil

1 medium yellow onion, finely chopped

1 large carrot, cut in ¼-in. (.5cm) dice (¾ cup)

1 or 2 medium stalks celery, cut in ¼-in. (.5cm) dice (¾ cup)

1 small parsnip, cut in ¼-in. (.5cm) dice (½ cup)

1 clove garlic, minced

1 tsp. kosher salt

4 cups *Golden Chicken-y Stock* or vegetable stock

1 tsp. nutritional yeast

½ tsp. reduced-sodium tamari

¼ tsp. freshly ground black pepper

1 TB. finely chopped fresh Italian flat-leaf parsley

1 TB. finely chopped fresh dill

For *Hearty Chicken-y and Rice Soup*, add 1 cup shredded or cubed seitan when you add vegetable stock, and use 2 cups freshly cooked rice instead of cooked pasta. Once you've added your starch, serve immediately, or it will "drink" up all the stock. If you're making this in advance, or you're planning to freeze a batch, add pasta or rice just before serving. If you don't have time to make homemade stock, choose a low- or no-salt boxed vegetable stock over bouillons or pastes, as these are salty and frequently unpleasant tasting.

Ginger Kale Soup

The flavors of this soup are perfect—just enough ginger and garlic to stand up to the hearty kale and shiitakes, but light and gentle enough for someone who isn't feeling well.

YIELD 10 CUPS   SERVING 1 OR 2 CUPS   PREP 10 MINS   COOK 25 MINS

1 In a medium saucepan over medium-high heat, heat sesame oil. Add ginger, garlic, and white parts of scallions, and stir for 1 minute.

2 Add carrot and celery, and stir for 1 minute.

3 Add vegetable stock, tamari, and dried shiitake mushrooms, and simmer soup for 15 minutes.

4 Add fresh shiitake mushrooms and kale, and simmer, covered, for 5 minutes.

5 Remove dried shiitake mushrooms (compost them, or save them in the freezer for stock), and remove the pan from heat. Add lemon juice and a little Sriracha (if using).

6 Divide basmati rice among 4 bowls, and ladle soup over top. Garnish each bowl with reserved green scallion slices, and serve.

INGREDIENTS

1 TB. sesame oil

1 (2-in.; 5cm) piece fresh ginger, peeled and finely chopped (2 TB.)

3 cloves garlic, peeled and finely chopped

4 scallions, thinly sliced, white and green parts separated

1 large carrot, peeled and thinly sliced

2 large stalks celery, thinly sliced

8 cups vegetable stock

1 tsp. tamari

4 dried shiitake mushrooms, rinsed well

6 oz. (170g) fresh shiitake mushrooms, stems removed, and thinly sliced

8 leaves lacinato kale, stemmed and sliced into thin ribbons

Juice of 1 lemon (2 TB.)

1 tsp. Sriracha, or to taste (optional)

2 cups cooked basmati or jasmine rice

This soup is perfect for a winter cold. Ginger is a natural anti-inflammatory and painkiller; garlic has antibiotic properties; and shiitakes are valued for their immune system support, iron, and B vitamins and are used in Eastern medicine to cure headaches. Scallions and kale are rich in phytonutrients and help cleanse the blood, while rice is gentle on an upset stomach.

MUSHROOMS

The chewy texture and umami flavor of mushrooms—from simple white button mushrooms, to heartier cremini (baby bella) and portobello, to delicate chanterelles, to full-flavored varieties such as hen of the woods—easily stand in for meat. **Benefits** Anti-inflammatory, promote good gut bacteria, anticancer properties, good source of vitamin D. **Uses** Choose fresh mushrooms free of dried ends. Eat fresh in salads, cooked in dishes, or whole in burgers. **Recipes** Truffled Mushroom Pâté; Bánh Mì Portobello Burgers; Mushroom, Spinach, and Shallot Quiche; Oyster Mushroom Po'boys; Mushroom Barley Soup.

Mushroom Barley Soup Ⓣ

Fortifying Polish mushroom barley soup, or *krupnik,* contains fresh and dried mushrooms, pearl barley, and root vegetables. Dried *borowik* mushrooms lend an authentic flavor if you can find them. Otherwise, try porcini or dried forest mix mushrooms.

YIELD 10 CUPS   SERVING 2 CUPS   PREP 20 MINS   COOK 70 MINS

1   In a small saucepan over medium heat, bring 1 cup vegetable stock to a simmer.

2   Rinse dried mushrooms, place in a small bowl, and pour hot stock over top. Set aside to soften for 10 minutes.

3   When mushrooms are softened, lift them out of stock, gently agitating to loosen any remaining soil, and lightly squeeze dry and finely chop. Reserve mushroom soaking liquid.

4   In a large, heavy soup pot over medium heat, heat grapeseed oil. Add yellow onions, celery, and carrots, and cook, stirring frequently, for 10 minutes.

5   Add chopped dried mushrooms, garlic, and button mushrooms, and cook for 5 minutes.

6   Line a fine-mesh strainer with cheesecloth, and pour reserved mushroom soaking liquid through the strainer into the soup pot. Add remaining 8 cups vegetable stock, increase heat to high, and bring to a boil.

7   Stir in pearl barley, yellow potatoes, bay leaf, 2 tablespoons Italian flat-leaf parsley, kosher salt, and black pepper. Reduce heat to medium-low, and cook for about 45 more minutes or until barley and vegetables are tender.

8   Remove soup from heat, and remove bay leaf. Stir in lemon juice and remaining 2 tablespoons Italian flat-leaf parsley, taste to see if soup needs more salt, and serve hot. Soup will keep in the refrigerator for up to 5 days.

INGREDIENTS

9 cups vegetable stock

1 oz. (25g) dried borowik, porcini, or forest mix mushrooms

2 TB. grapeseed oil

2 large yellow onions, finely chopped (3 cups)

4 small stalks celery, finely chopped (1 cup)

2 small carrots, finely chopped (1 cup)

3 cloves garlic, finely chopped

12 oz. (340g) button mushrooms, thinly sliced

¾ cup pearl barley

4 medium yellow potatoes (such as Yukon gold), peeled and cut in ½-in. (1.25cm) dice

1 bay leaf

4 TB. finely chopped fresh Italian flat-leaf parsley

1 tsp. kosher salt, plus more to taste

½ tsp. freshly ground black pepper

Juice of ½ medium lemon (1 TB.)

If you're making a big batch of soup for the freezer, leave out the potato (which will become mealy when thawed) and increase the barley by ½ cup. The soup will keep for up to 3 months when frozen in an airtight container. Don't forget to leave 1 inch (2.5cm) headspace to account for expansion when the soup freezes.

Curried Cauliflower Coconut Soup

Creamy cauliflower is accented with warm spices, coconut milk, and fresh lime juice in this soup. The sunny color and bright flavors make it the perfect choice to simmer on a rainy afternoon.

YiELD 8 CUPS   SERViNG 1 CUP   PREP 10 MiNS   COOK 20 MiNS

1   In a medium soup pot over medium-high heat, heat grapeseed oil. Add yellow onion, carrot, celery, garlic, and kosher salt, and cook, stirring gently, for about 5 minutes or until onion is softened.

2   Add cauliflower and vegetable stock. Reduce heat to medium-low, cover, and cook for about 10 minutes or until cauliflower is tender.

3   Stir in coconut milk, curry powder, and sambal oelek, and cook for 2 more minutes.

4   Remove from heat, and stir in lime juice.

5   Using an immersion blender, purée soup until smooth, or transfer in batches to a blender to purée. Serve immediately, garnished with a few whole cilantro leaves.

INGREDiENTS

1 TB. grapeseed oil

1 medium yellow onion, finely chopped

1 large carrot, finely chopped (¾ cup)

2 medium stalks celery, finely chopped (½ cup)

1 clove garlic, minced

1 tsp. kosher salt

1 medium head cauliflower, cut into florets (about 4 or 5 cups)

4 cups vegetable stock

1 (15-oz.; 420g) can full-fat coconut milk

1 tsp. curry powder

½ tsp. sambal oelek (chili garlic paste)

Juice of ½ lime (1 tsp.)

Fresh cilantro leaves

If you have Jamaican or West Indian curry power, use it in this soup. Island curries contain allspice rather than cardamom like Indian curries do. The allspice gives this soup a warm, gentle curry flavor that works well with the sweet, nutty flavors of cauliflower and coconut milk. Indian curry makes a soup that's sharper tasting but still very good.

Smoky White Bean and Tomato Soup

Protein-packed white beans are cooked with garlic and fragrant rosemary and enhanced with tomatoes, smoked sea salt, and aromatic vegetables in this easy soup. Soak the beans for at least 6 hours beforehand to shorten the cook time and produce creamy, evenly cooked beans.

YiELD 12 CUPS   **SERViNG** 1 OR 2 CUPS   **PREP** 10 MiNS   **COOK** 40 TO 60 MiNUTES

1   Drain soaked great northern beans, rinse well, and place in a large soup pot. Cover with vegetable stock, add garlic, rosemary, and thyme, and bring to a boil over high heat. Reduce heat to a simmer, and cook, partially covered, for 30 minutes. Taste beans for tenderness; they should be almost completely cooked but slightly al dente at this point. If not, cook for 10 to 15 more minutes.

2   Place tomato paste in a small bowl, and ladle in a little of the hot stock. Stir well, and add tomato paste mixture, smoked sea salt, kosher salt, yellow onion, celery, tomatoes with juice, ¼ cup extra-virgin olive oil, crushed red pepper flakes, and black pepper. Increase heat to high, and return to a boil. Reduce heat to medium-low, and simmer, uncovered, for 30 minutes or until beans are completely tender.

3   Remove from heat, and stir in apple cider vinegar and remaining 2 tablespoons olive oil. If desired, remove ½ cup soup to a blender, purée, return to the pot, and stir (or use an immersion blender to purée slightly). Serve hot. Soup will keep in the refrigerator for several days and can be frozen for up to 3 months.

INGREDiENTS

2 cups dry great northern beans or other small white beans, soaked 6 hours or overnight

8 cups vegetable stock or filtered water

4 cloves garlic, thinly sliced

1 TB. finely chopped fresh rosemary

1 tsp. finely chopped fresh thyme or ½ tsp. dried

¼ cup tomato paste

1 tsp. smoked sea salt

1 tsp. kosher salt

1 large yellow onion, chopped (about 1½ cups)

4 small stalks celery, cut in ¼-in. (.5cm) dice (1 cup)

1 (28-oz.; 800g) can diced tomatoes, with juice

¼ cup plus 2 TB. extra-virgin olive oil

¼ tsp. crushed red pepper flakes

¼ tsp. freshly ground black pepper

1 TB. apple cider vinegar

The success of this recipe relies on the flavor the beans both absorb and create as they cook. Be sure your beans are fresh and well soaked for best results. "Old" beans can take forever to cook. Canned beans won't provide the same result. However, if you must have them, reduce the water to 8 cups, and combine the beans, water, tomatoes, vegetables, extra-virgin olive oil, and spices, and simmer for about 20 minutes or until vegetables are tender.

Black pepper

Classic Vegetable Soup

This comforting soup comes together very quickly. With one spoonful of this flavorful tomato vegetable broth full of chunky veggies and alphabet pasta letters, you'll instantly be transported back in time. Add a peanut butter and jelly sandwich for the perfect nostalgic lunch!

YIELD 8 CUPS   SERVING 1 CUP   PREP 10 MINS   COOK 20 MINS

1 Bring a pot of water to a boil over medium-high heat, add alphabet pasta, and cook according to the package directions. Drain and set aside.

2 In a medium soup pot over medium-high heat, heat grapeseed oil. Add yellow onion, celery, red bell pepper, garlic, and kosher salt, and cook, stirring frequently, for about 5 minutes or until softened.

3 Add allspice, vegetable stock, tomato-vegetable juice, and frozen mixed vegetables, and bring to a boil. Reduce heat to medium, and cook, partially covered, for 10 minutes.

4 Stir in cooked pasta and lemon juice, cook for 1 minute or until pasta is heated through, and serve.

INGREDIENTS

¾ cup alphabet pasta

1 tsp. grapeseed oil

1 medium yellow onion, finely chopped

2 large stalks celery, finely chopped (½ cup)

¼ large red bell pepper, finely chopped (¼ cup)

1 clove garlic, minced

1 tsp. kosher salt

¼ tsp. ground allspice

4 cups vegetable stock

2 cups tomato-vegetable juice

2 cups frozen mixed vegetables (green beans, peas, carrots, corn)

Juice of ½ lemon (1 TB.)

This soup is very mild in flavor, making it perfect for children, for whom complex flavors are overwhelming and sometimes unpleasant. If you want a more grown-up version, add as many fresh vegetables as you like, use black pepper and hot sauce, or add more spices to the pot when you sauté the veggies.

Tomato Rice Soup

There's nothing nicer on a cold day than a bowl of hot tomato rice soup. This gently spiced comfort food classic comes together quickly but tastes like it simmered all day. Make a double batch, and put some in the freezer for easy meals later.

YIELD 8 CUPS   SERVING 1 CUP   PREP 10 MINS   COOK 20 MINS

1 In a medium soup pot over medium-high heat, heat extra-virgin olive oil. Add leeks, carrot, and celery, and cook for about 5 minutes or until leek is reduced and softened.

2 Add garlic, kosher salt, sweet Hungarian paprika, black pepper, smoked paprika, allspice, cloves, and bay leaf, and stir for 1 minute.

3 Add crushed tomatoes with juice and vegetable stock, bring to a boil, and stir in white basmati rice. Reduce heat to medium, cover, and cook, stirring occasionally, for 15 minutes or until rice is tender.

4 Remove bay leaf, and stir in white wine and hot sauce (if using). Serve immediately, or freeze in an airtight container for up to 3 months.

INGREDIENTS

3 TB. extra-virgin olive oil

2 medium leeks, thinly sliced (4 cups)

1 large carrot, finely chopped (¾ cup)

4 medium stalks celery, finely chopped (1 cup)

2 cloves garlic, finely chopped

1 tsp. kosher salt

1 tsp. sweet Hungarian paprika

½ tsp. freshly ground black pepper

¼ tsp. smoked paprika

¼ tsp. ground allspice

¼ tsp. ground cloves

1 bay leaf

1 (28-oz.; 800g) can plum tomatoes, with juice, crushed by hand

4 cups vegetable stock or filtered water

½ cup white basmati rice

¼ cup dry white wine

½ tsp. hot sauce (optional)

If you prefer the added fiber and nutritional value of brown rice, you can replace the white basmati rice with 1 cup cooked brown rice, added during the last 5 minutes of cooking.

Mushroom and Cabbage Borscht

This sweet and sour Ukrainian standard is made throughout Eastern and Central Europe with many variations. It's equally good served steaming hot in cold weather as it is chilled and topped with a dollop of plant-based sour cream on a warm summer day.

YiELD 10 TO 12 CUPS   **SERVING** 1 OR 2 CUPS   **PREP** 10 MiNS   **COOK** 70 MiNS

1   Preheat the oven to 400°F (200°C).

2   Scrub beets, but do not peel. Roast beets on a baking sheet lined with parchment paper for about 30 minutes or until tender. Cool slightly, peel, and cut into ¼-inch (.5cm) dice. (Beets can be roasted 1 day in advance.)

3   In a large soup pot over medium-high heat, heat remaining 1 tablespoon grapeseed oil. Add yellow onions, carrots, celery, button mushrooms, sugar, and kosher salt. Cook, stirring frequently, for 5 to 10 minutes or until onions are softened and vegetables begin to color.

4   Stir in black pepper and tomato paste. Add mushroom stock and reserved beets. Increase heat to high, bring to a boil, and stir in savoy cabbage. Reduce heat to medium-low, and cook, partially covered, stirring occasionally, for about 30 minutes or until cabbage is tender.

5   Remove from heat, stir in lemon juice and fresh dill, and serve. Leftovers will keep in the refrigerator for 3 days and can be served hot or cold.

INGREDIENTS

4 small beets

1 TB. plus 1 tsp. grapeseed oil

2 medium yellow onions, halved and thinly sliced

2 medium carrots, thinly sliced

3 large stalks celery, thinly sliced

1 (10-oz.; 285g) pkg. white button mushrooms, thinly sliced

1 TB. sugar

2 tsp. kosher salt

¼ tsp. freshly ground black pepper

2 TB. tomato paste

8 cups mushroom stock

1 small head savoy cabbage, shredded (about 6 cups)

2 TB. freshly squeezed lemon juice, or apple cider vinegar

¼ cup finely chopped fresh dill

When you have time to cook a full meal, make a double batch and freeze it. I love taking a quart of soup or pasta sauce out of the freezer in the morning, knowing all I have to do when I come home from work is cook some pasta or heat my soup, and toss together a green salad.

Split-Pea Soup

Smoked sea salt is the secret to creating the smoky flavor that characterizes an excellent pea soup. This split-pea soup is thick, but not too thick, and perfectly seasoned with a long-cooked flavor.

YIELD 12 CUPS **SERVING** 1 OR 2 CUPS **PREP** 15 MINS **COOK** 40 TO 60 MINS

1 Pick over split peas, removing any small stones or debris. Rinse well, and set aside.

2 In a large soup pot over medium-high heat, heat extra-virgin olive oil. Add yellow onion, carrots, celery, garlic, smoked sea salt, kosher salt, thyme, and sage. Reduce heat to medium, and cook, stirring frequently, for 5 minutes or until vegetables are softened.

3 Add split peas, vegetable stock, 4 cups filtered water, cayenne, and crushed red pepper, and cook, stirring frequently, for about 30 more minutes or until peas are mushy and broken down.

4 Stir in black pepper, white wine, and lemon juice. Remove from heat, and purée with an immersion blender or in batches in a blender. Add more water if needed to thin to desired consistency, and taste and add more kosher salt or black pepper if necessary.

5 Serve hot. Pea soup will keep in the freezer in an airtight container for up to 3 months.

INGREDIENTS

4 cups split peas (green, yellow, or a mix of both, about 1½ lb.; 680g)

2 TB. extra-virgin olive oil

1 large yellow onion, chopped (about 1½ cups)

2 medium carrots, cut in ¼-in. (.5cm) dice (1 cup)

4 medium stalks celery, cut in ¼-in. (.5cm) dice (1 cup)

2 cloves garlic, minced

1 tsp. smoked sea salt

½ tsp. kosher salt

½ tsp. dried thyme

½ tsp. crumbled dried sage

6 cups vegetable stock

4 to 6 cups filtered water

Pinch cayenne

Pinch crushed red pepper flakes

¼ tsp. freshly ground black pepper

¼ cup dry white wine

Juice of 1 lemon (2 TB.)

While your soup is simmering, make *Croutons*. Preheat the oven to 400°F (200°C). Cut 3 or 4 slices of rye or pumpernickel bread into ¼-inch (.5cm) cubes. Melt 2 tablespoons plant-based butter and toss with bread, 1 pinch salt, and 1 pinch cayenne. Spread on a parchment paper–lined baking sheet, and bake, stirring frequently, for 10 minutes or until croutons are brown and crispy. Store leftovers in an airtight container for up to 1 week.

Split green peas

Creamy Corn Chowder

Almonds lend a creamy consistency to this delicious soup, which is brimming with potatoes, corn, and aromatic vegetables.

YIELD 8 OR 9 CUPS **SERVING** 2 CUPS **PREP** 10 MINS **COOK** 20 MINS PLUS OVERNIGHT SOAK TIME

1 Soak almonds in cold water overnight.

2 Discard water nuts soaked in, rinse nuts well, and drain. Set aside.

3 In a large soup pot over medium heat, heat extra-virgin olive oil. Add yellow onion, and cook, stirring frequently, for 5 minutes.

4 Add celery, red bell pepper, carrot, and kosher salt, and cook for 3 more minutes or until vegetables are softened and just beginning to color.

5 Add all-purpose flour, and stir for 1 minute.

6 Add vegetable stock, stirring vigorously to combine. Bring to a boil, and reserve 1 cup stock. Add Yukon gold potatoes and corn.

7 In a blender, combine almonds and reserved vegetable stock, and blend until smooth. Stir almond mixture into soup, and simmer until potatoes are tender.

8 Add plant-based butter, lemon juice, hot sauce, and black pepper. Serve immediately.

INGREDIENTS

1 cup blanched almonds

2 TB. extra-virgin olive oil

1 large yellow onion, finely chopped (about 1½ cups)

2 small stalks celery, finely chopped (½ cup)

½ medium red bell pepper, finely chopped (½ cup)

1 medium carrot, finely chopped (½ cup)

1 tsp. kosher salt

2 TB. all-purpose flour

6 cups light vegetable stock

3 large Yukon gold potatoes, peeled and cut into ¼-in. (.5cm) dice (2 cups)

6 cups corn kernels (shucked from about 4 ears corn)

1 TB. plant-based butter

1 tsp. freshly squeezed lemon juice

½ tsp. hot sauce, such as Sriracha

¼ tsp. freshly ground black pepper

For *Gluten-Free Corn Chowder,* omit flour. When potatoes are tender, whisk 2 tablespoons cornstarch with 2 tablespoons cold water until smooth and stir into soup to thicken.

Beans and Legumes

Beans pack a lot of protein in a small package. Chickpeas are the basis of hummus, and many dried beans add nutrition to soups, stews, burgers, and more. When shopping for dried beans, buy them in bulk bins or in bags, and avoid broken or shriveled beans when possible. Soak dried beans overnight, or quick-soak them by boiling for 10 minutes and soaking for 1 hour. Rinse, drain, and proceed with the recipe.

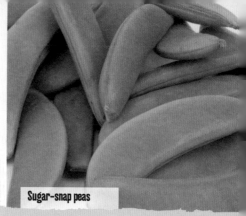

Sugar-snap peas

Fresh Beans

	FRENCH BEANS (haricot verts)	GARDEN PEAS	LiMA BEANS (butter, broad)	POLE BEANS (snap, wax, green, string)	SNOW PEAS	SUGAR-SNAP PEAS
USES	Lightly steam or blanch slender, firm, dark green beans. Or sauté or toss with vinaigrette.	Opt for unshelled fresh peas, shell them yourself, and blanch or steam for 2 or 3 minutes. Drizzle with olive oil, salt, and pepper. Add fresh herbs such as tarragon, chives, parsley, or chervil.	Opt for unshelled beans with firm, dark green pods. Steam or blanch shelled beans for 5 minutes. Use in vegetable soups or stews, or sauté.	Steam, blanch, or stir-fry firm, crisp, brightly colored beans. Use in salads and vegetable soups, or sauté or roast.	Choose light green, firm, smooth pods with small peas visible inside. Scrub well, and pull the stringlike fiber from one end to remove. Serve raw, steamed, blanched, sautéed, or stir-fried.	Choose chubby, firm pods with a bright green color. Scrub well, pull the stringlike fiber from one end to remove, and cut off both ends. Add to stir-fries, salads, or soups.
GOOD SOURCE OF ...	Antioxidants; fiber; vitamins K, C, B_2, B_1; folate; and iron.	Protein; phytonutrients; antioxidants; omega-3 fats; fiber; manganese; copper; phosphorus; folate; vitamins K, B_1, B_2, B_3, B_6; iron; and potassium.	Protein, fiber, copper, manganese, folate, iron, potassium, phosphorus, and vitamins B_1 and B_6.	Antioxidants; fiber; vitamins K, C, B_2, B_1; folate; and iron.	Fiber; riboflavin; vitamins B_6, A, C, K; magnesium; phosphorus; potassium; fiber; thiamin; folate; iron; and manganese.	Fiber, vitamins C and K, iron, magnesium, phosphorus, potassium, and antioxidants.

French beans

Peas

Black-eyed peas

Peanuts

Dried Beans and Legumes

	BLACK-EYED PEAS (cow peas)	CHICKPEAS	KIDNEY BEANS	LENTILS (brown, green, red)	MUNG BEANS (gram)	PEANUTS	SOYBEANS
USES	Pair with collards or kale, potatoes, smoked salt or paprika, corn, summer squash, lima beans, garlic, onions, and tomatoes.	Use in salads, burgers, soups, stews, and pasta dishes.	Enjoy in chilies, soups, stews, and salads.	Lentils don't need soaking, and cook quickly. Green lentils are firm and best in soups and salads. Brown lentils are tender and good in soups, stews, and as a ground beef substitute. Red lentils are best in soups and purées.	Pair with coconut, curries, soups, stews, garlic, onions, and ginger.	Enjoy as a snack, or use in sauces or stews. Pair with strong flavors such as ginger and garlic.	Use in burgers, soups, stews, or purées.
GOOD SOURCE OF ...	Protein, fiber, vitamins A and K, B vitamins, and potassium.	Protein, fiber, copper, folate, and manganese.	Protein, vitamin B_6, pantothenic acid, iron, magnesium, phosphorus, potassium, vitamin C, thiamin, riboflavin, niacin, folate, copper, and manganese.	Protein, iron, phosphorus, copper, fiber, folate, and manganese.	Protein, fiber, vitamin C, thiamin, folate, calcium, magnesium, phosphorus, potassium, and manganese.	Protein, fiber, niacin, manganese, iron, and calcium.	Protein, fiber, vitamin C, thiamin, folate, calcium, magnesium, phosphorus, potassium, and manganese.

Chickpeas

Lentils

Tom Yum Soup

Tom yum has an addictive flavor that's tart, tangy, and spicy all at once, with the exotic flavors of lemongrass, galangal (Thai ginger), Kaffir lime, and plenty of hot chiles. It's surprisingly comforting, wonderful to eat when you're suffering from a cold.

YiELD 6 CUPS SERViNG 1½ CUPS PREP 15 MiNS COOK 10 MiNS

1 Peel tough outer layer from lemongrass stalks, and smash stalks with the flat side of your knife to tenderize. Chop finely.

2 In a medium saucepan over medium-high heat, heat coconut oil. Add lemongrass, galangal, Kaffir lime leaves, hot red chile pepper, and sambal oelek, and stir for 1 minute.

3 Add Golden Chicken-y Stock, button mushrooms, tofu, and tamari, and bring to a boil.

4 Reduce heat to medium, and cook for 10 minutes or until mushrooms are tender.

5 Remove from heat, remove and discard lime leaves, stir in lime juice and cilantro, and serve. Soup can be made 1 day in advance. Add lime juice and cilantro just before serving.

INGREDiENTS

2 large stalks fresh lemongrass

1 tsp. coconut oil or grapeseed oil

2 TB. finely chopped galangal or ginger

3 Kaffir lime leaves, fresh or frozen, or the zest of 1 medium lime

1 small fresh hot red chile pepper, such as Thai bird chile or Serrano, thinly sliced

2 tsp. sambal oelek (chili garlic sauce)

5 cups *Golden Chicken-y Stock* or vegetable stock

6 oz. (170g) white button mushrooms, sliced

¼ lb. (115g) firm silken tofu, cut in ½-in. (1.25cm) cubes

2 TB. reduced-sodium tamari

Juice of 1½ medium limes (2 TB.)

¼ cup finely chopped fresh cilantro

Tom yum is traditionally made with Thai chile paste, an ingredient that almost always contains shrimp paste or fish sauce. A quick online search yields dozens of recipes for homemade vegetarian versions of Thai chile paste, so if you like this recipe and want to create something more authentic, you can try making your own at home. If you don't want a very spicy soup, add half of a 14-ounce (400g) can of full-fat coconut milk, and reduce the amount of sambal oelek to 1 teaspoon, or to taste. To reduce the heat factor more, you also can halve the fresh chile, sauté it, and remove it before serving.

Miso Udon Bowl

Miso soup makes a nourishing meal with the addition of mushrooms, tofu, tender baby spinach, and hearty udon noodles.

YIELD 8 CUPS   SERVING 2 CUPS   PREP 5 MINS   COOK 20 MINS

1   Cook udon noodles in boiling water according to the package directions. Drain in a colander, rinse with cold water, and set aside.

2   In a small saucepan over medium-high heat, heat kombu stock until simmering.

3   In a medium saucepan over medium-high heat, heat grapeseed oil. Add shiitake mushrooms, and sauté for 1 minute.

4   Add ginger and garlic, and sauté for 30 seconds. Add heated stock, bring to a boil, and reduce heat to a simmer. Stir in wakame and tofu, and cook for 5 minutes.

5   Ladle ½ cup soup into a small bowl, and whisk in white (shiro) miso paste.

6   Stir baby spinach and noodles into soup, and cook for 1 minute or until spinach is wilted. Remove from heat and stir in miso mixture. Serve immediately.

INGREDIENTS

1 (8-oz.; 225g) pkg. udon noodles

4 cups kombu stock or vegetable stock

1 tsp. grapeseed oil

1 (4-oz.; 100g) pkg. shiitake mushrooms, stemmed and thinly sliced (about 1½ cups)

1 (1-in.; 2.5cm) piece fresh ginger, finely grated (2 TB.)

1 clove garlic, minced

1 cup wakame (seaweed)

½ pkg. firm silken tofu, cut into ½-in. (1.25cm) cubes

2 TB. white (shiro) miso paste

1 (5-oz.; 140g) pkg. baby spinach

For *Quick Miso Soup,* heat 1 cup kombu or vegetable stock per serving. Ladle 1/2 cup simmering stock into a small bowl, and stir in 1 teaspoon white miso paste per serving. If desired, add a 1/4 cup cubed tofu per serving to the soup as it simmers.

GINGER

Ginger is an ancient root spice with hot and tangy flavor that pairs well with chiles, coconut, garlic, limes, and green onions. It can alleviate many types of pain and inflammation. **Benefits** Anti-inflammatory, aids digestive health, antinausea, increases absorption of nutrients. **Uses** Choose fresh whole roots or frozen as a paste, and use in Asian dishes, juice with fresh fruits and vegetables, or add to baked goods. **Recipes** Ginger Kale Soup, Sesame Ginger Broccoli, Lentil and Vegetable Dal, Triple Ginger Molasses Cookies, Pumpkin Gingerbread Cupcakes.

Meaty Mushroom Stew

This mushroom stew is rich, meaty-tasting, and delicious, thanks to a mix of mushrooms, including hen of the woods, which lend a chicken-y texture and incredible flavor to this cold-weather delight.

YIELD 8 CUPS   SERVING 1 CUP   PREP 15 MINS   COOK 30 MINS

1   In a 4-quart (4L) stock pot over medium-high heat, heat 2 tablespoons extra-virgin olive oil. Add yellow onions and shallot, and cook, stirring frequently, for 5 minutes.

2   Add celery, carrot, white button mushrooms, hen of the woods mushrooms, chanterelle mushrooms, and garlic, and cook, stirring frequently, for about 10 minutes or until mushrooms begin to turn golden. Add remaining 2 tablespoons olive oil as mushrooms begin to stick to the pan.

3   Stir in kosher salt, black pepper, sweet Hungarian paprika, thyme, and dill.

4   Add all-purpose flour to mushroom mixture, and stir for 2 minutes.

5   Add 3 cups Mushroom Stock, red wine, and russet potato, and bring to a boil. Reduce heat to medium, and cook, stirring often, for 10 minutes or until stew is thickened and vegetables are tender. Add additional stock if stew is too thick for your liking.

6   Remove from heat, and stir in Italian flat-leaf parsley and balsamic vinegar. Taste, add more kosher salt and black pepper if needed, and serve. Stew will keep in the refrigerator for up to 5 days and is even more delicious the next day.

INGREDIENTS

4 TB. extra-virgin olive oil

2 medium yellow onions, finely chopped (about 2½ cups)

1 small shallot, halved and finely chopped

2 medium stalks celery, finely chopped (1 cup)

1 large carrot, finely chopped (1 cup)

1 (10-oz.; 285g) pkg. tiny white button mushrooms, halved

8 oz. (225g) hen of the woods mushrooms, sliced

8 oz. (225g) fresh chanterelle mushrooms, sliced

3 cloves garlic, finely chopped

1 tsp. kosher salt, plus more to taste

½ tsp. freshly ground black pepper, plus more to taste

1 TB. sweet Hungarian paprika

1 tsp. dried thyme

1 tsp. dried dill

2 TB. all-purpose flour

3 or 4 cups *Mushroom Stock*

1 cup dry red wine

1 large russet potato, peeled and diced (1½ cups)

¼ cup finely chopped fresh Italian flat-leaf parsley

1 TB. balsamic vinegar

Feel free to experiment with different kinds of mushrooms in this stew—trumpet, oyster, morels, or even just cremini (baby bella) and shiitakes if you aren't on a wild mushroom budget. You also can substitute 2 ounces (55g) dried chanterelles if you can't find fresh, or you can use dried porcini instead.

Gumbo Filé (T)

Gumbo filé is an amazing Creole stew layered with flavor. Oyster mushrooms and veggie Andouille sausage swim in a fragrant, deliciously spiced, roux-thickened broth. The ingredient list seems long, but once your veggies are chopped and the spices are measured out, making this is a snap. Take the time to make it right, and everyone you feed will love you forever.

YIELD 10 CUPS   SERVING 2 CUPS   PREP 25 MINS   COOK 90 MINS

1   In a large soup pot over medium heat, heat grapeseed oil. Whisk in all-purpose flour until well combined. Using a wooden spoon, stir roux constantly over medium heat until mixture is a golden, caramel brown color.

2   Stir in yellow onion, celery, green bell pepper, and red bell pepper, and cook, stirring frequently, for 10 more minutes. Reduce heat to medium-low if necessary to prevent burning.

3   Add ½ of garlic, stir for 1 minute, and bring to a simmer.

4   Stir in vegetable stock, bring to a boil, and reduce heat to a gentle simmer.

5   Meanwhile, in a wide sauté pan over medium heat, heat extra-virgin olive oil. Add sliced veggie Andouille sausage, and stir for 1 minute. Using a slotted spoon, transfer sausage to a bowl.

6   Add oyster mushrooms and remaining garlic to the sauté pan, and stir until mushrooms are golden.

7   Add sweet paprika, kosher salt, Creole seasoning, oregano, thyme, black pepper, allspice, and cayenne, and stir for 1 minute.

8   Add amber beer, increase heat to high, and stir vigorously to deglaze the pan, releasing any browned bits stuck to the pan.

9   Stir mushroom mixture into soup pot along with fire-roasted tomatoes with juice, balsamic vinegar, vegan Worcestershire sauce, and hot sauce. Bring to a boil, reduce heat to low or medium-low, and simmer for 1 hour, stirring occasionally and adjusting heat as necessary.

10 Stir in reserved Andouille sausage and filé powder, and simmer for 5 minutes.

11 Stir in scallions, Italian flat-leaf parsley, and dark rum (if using). Ladle into bowls over hot, cooked rice, or serve with plenty of crusty French bread, passing additional filé powder and hot sauce at the table.

INGREDIENTS

½ cup grapeseed oil

½ cup all-purpose flour

1 large yellow onion, finely chopped (1½ cups)

4 medium stalks celery, finely chopped (2 cups)

1 medium green bell pepper, ribs and seeds removed, and finely chopped (1 cup)

1 medium red bell pepper, ribs and seeds removed, and finely chopped (1 cup)

6 cloves garlic, chopped

6 cups vegetable stock

¼ cup extra-virgin olive oil

2 links veggie Andouille sausage, thinly sliced

1 lb. (450g) oyster mushrooms, roughly chopped

1 tsp. sweet paprika

1 tsp. kosher salt

½ tsp. Creole seasoning

½ tsp. dried oregano

½ tsp. dried thyme

½ tsp. freshly ground black pepper

¼ tsp. ground allspice

Pinch cayenne

12 fl. oz. (350ml) amber beer

1 (14-oz.; 400g) can diced fire-roasted tomatoes, with juice

1 TB. balsamic vinegar

1 TB. vegan Worcestershire sauce, such as Annie's

1 tsp. Louisiana hot sauce, such as Crystal

2 tsp. filé powder, such as Tony Chachere's

½ cup thinly sliced scallions, white and green parts

¼ cup finely chopped fresh Italian flat-leaf parsley

2 TB. dark rum (optional)

Minestrone

A *minestre* is a soup thickened with beans, pasta, or even day-old country bread. Beans and potatoes thicken this hearty vegetable soup nicely. Minestrone makes a nourishing and comforting supper with the addition of nothing more than a loaf of good country bread and a simple green salad.

YIELD 10 CUPS   SERVING 2 CUPS   PREP 15 MINS   COOK 60 MINS

1   In a large soup pot over medium-high heat, heat 2 tablespoons extra-virgin olive oil. Add red onion, carrots, and celery, and cook, stirring often, for 5 minutes.

2   Add 2 cloves garlic, and stir for 1 minute more.

3   Stir in tomato paste, mix well, and add vegetable stock. Bring to a boil.

4   Add russet potato, bay leaf, and kosher salt. Reduce heat to a simmer, and cook for 15 minutes.

5   Meanwhile, in a wide sauté pan over medium-high heat, heat remaining 2 tablespoons extra-virgin olive oil. Add remaining 3 cloves garlic, and stir for 30 seconds.

6   Add savoy cabbage, and cook, stirring frequently, for about 10 minutes or until cabbage is softened.

7   Add cabbage to the soup pot along with cannellini beans, cranberry beans, tomatoes with juice, and 2 tablespoons Italian flat-leaf parsley, and simmer for 30 minutes.

8   Stir in red wine vinegar and black pepper. Allow soup to rest for 10 minutes, remove bay leaf, stir in remaining 2 tablespoons Italian flat-leaf parsley, and serve.

INGREDIENTS

4 TB. extra-virgin olive oil

1 large red onion, cut in small dice (2 cups)

3 medium carrots, cut in small dice (1½ cups)

4 large stalks celery, cut in small dice (1½ cups)

5 cloves garlic, minced

3 TB. tomato paste

6 cups vegetable stock

1 large russet potato, peeled and cut in small dice (1½ cups)

1 bay leaf

1 tsp. kosher salt, plus more to taste

½ small head savoy cabbage, thinly sliced (about 3 cups)

1 (14-oz.; 400g) can cannellini beans, rinsed and drained

1 (14-oz.; 400g) can cranberry beans, rinsed and drained

1 (28-oz.; 800g) can diced tomatoes, with juice

4 TB. finely chopped fresh Italian flat-leaf parsley

1 TB. red wine vinegar

½ tsp. freshly ground black pepper

Feel free to vary your minestrone seasonally based on what vegetables are fresh and available. For *Minestrone with Pasta,* eliminate the potato, increase the broth by 2 cups, and add 1 cup small pasta, such as ditalini, during the last 15 minutes of cooking. Leftover minestrone is wonderful hot or at room temperature. When my grandmother was a little girl, her father would stir the leftover vegetables and beans from a pot of minestrone into a pot of hot polenta, cool it in a baking dish, and cut it into wedges for the children to eat for lunch.

Carrots

Giambotta (Italian Summer Vegetable Stew)

My grandmother often made this summer vegetable stew with ingredients fresh from the garden, and it was amazing. Every Italian American family I know has their own way of making this tomato-based stew. Wait for late summer to make it, when tomatoes and peppers are sweet and zucchini and eggplant are in season.

YiELD 10 CUPS   **SERViNG** 2 CUPS   **PREP** 20 MiNS   **COOK** 60 MiNS

1 In a colander, toss eggplant with 1 teaspoon kosher salt, and set aside to drain over a bowl. After 30 minutes, discard liquid, rinse eggplant, and gently squeeze excess water from eggplant. Set aside.

2 Bring a medium pot of salted water to a boil over high heat. Add Italian green beans, and cook for 5 minutes. Using a slotted spoon, transfer beans to a bowl of ice water, immediately drain, and set aside.

3 In the same pot, cook white potatoes with boiling water to cover for about 15 minutes or until tender. Remove to a cutting board to cool slightly.

4 Meanwhile, core plum tomatoes and score a small X in the bottom of each.

5 When potatoes are done, using the same pot of boiling water and adding a little more if necessary, work in batches to quickly blanch tomatoes, about 1 minute at a time, transferring them to an ice bath immediately after. Peel tomatoes, seed, and cut into slices, reserving tomatoes and juice in a bowl.

6 In a 4-quart (4L) stock pot over medium-high heat, heat extra-virgin olive oil. Add yellow onions, and cook for 5 minutes.

7 Add garlic, and cook for 1 minute.

8 Stir in eggplant, and cook for another 5 minutes, stirring frequently to avoid vegetables sticking while cooking.

9 Stir in tomatoes, red bell peppers, zucchini, green beans, and remaining 1 teaspoon kosher salt, reduce heat to medium-low, and simmer for 20 minutes.

10 Meanwhile, peel potatoes and cut into quarters. When vegetables are tender, stir in potatoes and black pepper, and cook for 5 minutes. Remove from heat; and stir in basil; and serve hot, warm, or cold.

INGREDiENTS

1 medium eggplant, quartered and cut in ½-in. (1.25cm) slices

2 tsp. kosher salt

½ lb. (225g) flat Italian green beans, trimmed

3 large white potatoes, unpeeled

12 medium plum tomatoes

¼ cup extra-virgin olive oil

2 large yellow onions, halved and thinly sliced

2 cloves garlic, smashed and roughly chopped

2 red bell peppers, ribs and seeds removed, and thinly sliced

2 large zucchini, halved and thinly sliced

½ tsp. freshly ground black pepper

¼ cup fresh basil leaves

For *Vegetable Stew with Polenta,* eliminate potatoes and serve stew over hot, cooked polenta.

Lentil and Vegetable Dal

Lentil dal gets a makeover with the addition of cauliflower and spinach. Before you start making the dal, whip up a quick batch of dough for fresh naan, and you'll have an amazing feast ready in less than an hour.

YIELD 6 CUPS **SERVING** 1½ CUPS **PREP** 10 MINS **COOK** 30 MINS

1   In a large soup pot over medium-high heat, heat coconut oil. Add yellow onion, ginger, and garlic, and cook, stirring frequently, for 5 minutes. Reduce heat if necessary to prevent burning.

2   Stir in vegetable stock, red lentils, cauliflower, turmeric, coriander, cumin, cinnamon, and cayenne. Bring to a boil, reduce heat, and simmer for 20 minutes.

3   When lentils and cauliflower are tender, place tomato paste in a small bowl. Ladle a little bit of broth into the bowl, stir until smooth, and stir mixture back into the soup pot.

4   Add spinach, kosher salt, lime juice, and 1 tablespoon cilantro, and simmer for 5 minutes.

5   Whisk remaining 1 tablespoon cilantro into yogurt, and serve dal warm with a dollop of cilantro yogurt.

INGREDIENTS

2 TB. coconut oil

1 large yellow onion, finely chopped (1½ cups)

1 TB. finely chopped fresh ginger

2 cloves garlic, minced

6 cups vegetable stock

1 cup red lentils, picked over and rinsed

⅓ small head cauliflower, separated into florets and finely chopped (2 cups)

1 TB. ground turmeric

1 tsp. ground coriander

½ tsp. ground cumin

¼ tsp. ground cinnamon

¼ tsp. cayenne

2 TB. tomato paste

1 bunch spinach, washed well, stemmed, and thinly sliced

1 tsp. kosher salt

Juice of 1 medium lime (1 TB.)

2 TB. finely chopped fresh cilantro

½ cup plant-based plain yogurt

Make *Naan* to serve with dal. Before making dal, in a large bowl, whisk together 2½ cups all-purpose flour with 1 package fast-acting instant yeast, 2 teaspoons kosher salt, and 1 teaspoon baking powder. In a medium bowl, whisk together ¾ cup warm water, 3 tablespoons plain plant-based yogurt, and 2 tablespoons melted coconut oil. Stir wet ingredients into dry, and knead with your hands for 1 or 2 minutes to form sticky dough. Let dough rise at room temperature for 45 minutes or until doubled. 10 minutes before serving, heat a large cast-iron frying pan over medium heat. Divide dough into 6 balls and stretch into teardrop shapes about 5 inches (12.5cm) long. Dampen dough with a little water, add to the hot pan a few at a time, and cook for about 1 minute per side. Brush the pan with ½ teaspoon grapeseed oil to keep naan from sticking if necessary.

Green Curry Vegetable Stew

There's something special about the fragrance and flavor of green curry spices, Kaffir lime, ginger, and coconut milk, and the bounty of vegetables in this dish is so good for you. Treat yourself to a steaming bowl of this wonderful, fragrant stew as often as you can.

YIELD 6 CUPS   SERVING 2 CUPS   PREP 10 MINS   COOK 20 MINS

1   In a large saucepan over medium-high heat, heat virgin coconut oil. Add garlic, ginger, Thai green curry paste, and hot chile pepper, and stir for 1 minute.

2   Add yellow onion, shiitake mushrooms, and kosher salt, and stir for 2 minutes more.

3   Stir in coconut milk, vegetable stock, Kaffir lime leaves, and carrot. Bring to a boil, reduce heat to a simmer, and cook for 5 minutes.

4   Stir in zucchini, and simmer for 5 minutes.

5   Stir in baby spinach, scallion, and cilantro, and cook for 1 more minute. Remove from heat, and serve.

INGREDIENTS

2 TB. virgin coconut oil

2 cloves garlic, finely chopped

1 (1- or 2-in.; 2.5 to 5cm) piece ginger, peeled and grated (1 or 2 TB.)

2 TB. Thai green curry paste

1 hot chile pepper, such as Serrano, seeded and thinly sliced

1 medium yellow onion, halved and thinly sliced

1 (8-oz.; 225g) pkg. shiitake mushrooms, stemmed and thinly sliced

1 tsp. kosher salt, plus more to taste

1 (14-oz.; 400g) can full-fat, best-quality Thai coconut milk

1 cup vegetable stock or water

2 Kaffir lime leaves, or 1 TB. grated lime zest

1 cup carrot, thinly sliced

1 large zucchini, halved and thinly sliced

1 (10-oz.; 285g) pkg. baby spinach

½ cup thinly sliced scallion, white and light green parts

¼ cup finely chopped fresh cilantro

chiles

This stew is easy to vary. Use button mushrooms instead of shiitakes, or try red curry paste instead of green. Add baby bok choy, sautéed eggplant, daikon radish, or burdock root, or stir in cubed firm tofu with carrot. For a *Green Curry Dinner*, serve stew over hot, cooked rice or rice noodles.

Hearty Chilli Ⓣ ㉚

I come from a family who loves chili, and making a pot on a snowy day is almost standard for us. My version of this family favorite is full of beans, mushrooms, peppers, onions, and tomatoes, with a bit of a kick from habanero pepper sauce.

YIELD 12 CUPS   **SERVING** 2 CUPS   **PREP** 10 MINS   **COOK** 45 MINS

1   In a large stock pot over medium heat, heat extra-virgin olive oil. Add yellow onions, red bell peppers, and yellow bell peppers, and cook, stirring often, for 10 minutes.

2   Stir in cremini mushrooms, garlic, kosher salt, chili powder, cumin, Anaheim chile powder, oregano, and black pepper, and cook, stirring frequently, for 10 minutes.

3   Add tomatoes with juice, stir, and bring to a boil. Reduce heat to low or medium low, and cook at a gently bubbling simmer, uncovered, for about 30 minutes or until peppers and onions are very tender.

4   Stir in kidney beans, black beans, and habanero hot sauce, and cook for 5 minutes. Serve in big bowls with a spoonful of plant-based sour cream (if using) and plenty of tortilla chips (if using).

INGREDIENTS

¼ cup extra-virgin olive oil

2 large yellow onions, diced (3 cups)

4 medium red bell peppers, ribs and seeds removed, and diced

2 medium yellow bell peppers, ribs and seeds removed, and diced

1 (10-oz.; 285g) pkg. cremini (baby bella) mushrooms, thinly sliced

4 cloves garlic, finely chopped

1 tsp. kosher salt

2 TB. chili powder

1 tsp. ground cumin

1 tsp. Anaheim chile powder

1 tsp. dried oregano

1 tsp. freshly ground black pepper

2 (28-oz.; 800g) cans diced tomatoes, with juice

2 (14-oz.; 400g) cans kidney beans, rinsed and drained

2 (14-oz.; 400g) cans black beans, rinsed and drained

1 TB. habanero hot sauce, such as El Yucateco, plus more for serving

Plant-based sour cream (optional)

Tortilla chips (optional)

My mom adds about ¼ cup tequila to her chili during the last 5 minutes of cooking. It adds that delicious, "What is that ingredient?" flavor. Try it if you're not serving your chili to minors or pregnant women.

Black-Eyed Pea Stew

The "Holy Trinity" of Louisiana cooking—celery, onions, and bell pepper—provides the flavor base in this tomato-rich, Creole-style stew, while a little veggie Andouille sausage pumps up the protein content and spice.

YiELD 8 CUPS   SERViNG 1 CUP   PREP 10 MiNS   COOK 20 MiNS

1   In a large saucepan over medium-high heat, heat extra-virgin olive oil. Add sweet onion, celery, and green bell pepper, and cook, stirring frequently and adjusting heat as necessary, for 5 minutes.

2   Stir in veggie Andouille sausage, and cook for 2 minutes.

3   Add garlic, Creole seasoning, kosher salt, and black pepper, and stir for 1 minute.

4   Stir in diced tomatoes with juice, red wine, and black-eyed peas. Reduce heat to medium, and cook, stirring frequently, for 10 minutes.

5   When vegetables are tender, remove from heat; stir in Italian flat-leaf parsley, apple cider vinegar, and hot sauce; and serve.

The level of heat in Andouille sausage varies, so if you're sensitive to spice, you might want to reduce the Creole seasoning or hot sauce. Taste and adjust as you cook. You can serve this quick and easy stew over hot, cooked rice, or sop it up with some good, crusty French bread. All you need is a salad dressed with a simple vinaigrette, and dinner is served. The stew freezes well, so make a double batch. It will keep in the freezer for 3 months.

INGREDiENTS

2 TB. extra-virgin olive oil

1 large sweet onion, finely chopped (1½ cups)

3 medium stalks celery, finely chopped (1 cup)

1 large green bell pepper, ribs and seeds removed, and finely chopped (1 cup)

2 links veggie Andouille sausage, removed from casing (if necessary) and sliced or crumbled

3 cloves garlic, finely chopped

1 TB. Creole seasoning

1 tsp. kosher salt, plus more to taste

½ tsp. freshly ground black pepper, plus more to taste

1 (28-oz.; 800g) can diced tomatoes, with juice

1 cup dry red wine

2 (14-oz.; 400g) cans black-eyed peas, rinsed and drained

¼ cup finely chopped fresh Italian flat-leaf parsley

1 TB. apple cider vinegar

1 tsp. Louisiana hot sauce, such as Crystal

Jerusalem Artichoke Soup

Jerusalem artichokes, or sunchokes, combine the nutty flavor of an artichoke with the creamy consistency of a potato, making them perfect for this comforting soup.

YiELD 6 CUPS   **SERViNG** 1½ CUPS   **PREP** 15 MiNS   **COOK** 35 TO 45 MiNS

1 In a large soup pot over medium heat, heat virgin grapeseed oil. Add yellow onions, and cook, stirring frequently, for 5 to 10 minutes or until soft and translucent.

2 Add garlic, and cook for 30 seconds or until fragrant.

3 Stir in Jerusalem artichokes, carrots, and kosher salt, cover, reduce heat to low, and cook, stirring frequently, for 10 to 15 minutes or until vegetables are softened.

4 Add vegetable stock, thyme, and saffron. Bring to a boil, reduce heat to a simmer, and cook for 20 minutes or until vegetables are soft.

5 Cool briefly, and purée until smooth using an immersion blender or by transferring to a food processor or blender in batches if necessary.

6 Stir in lemon juice, season to taste with more kosher salt and black pepper, and serve in warm bowls with a drizzle of olive oil on top.

iNGREDiENTS

2 TB. virgin grapeseed oil or extra-virgin olive oil, plus more for garnish

2 medium yellow onions, chopped

3 cloves garlic, finely chopped

12 oz. (340g) Jerusalem artichokes, peeled or scrubbed well, and coarsely chopped

1 medium carrot, peeled and coarsely chopped

½ tsp. kosher salt, plus more to taste

5 cups hot vegetable stock

1 TB. chopped fresh thyme leaves, or 1½ tsp. dried

Large pinch (about 30 strands) saffron

Juice of ½ medium lemon (2 TB.)

¼ tsp. freshly ground black pepper, or to taste

Jerusalem artichokes

Posole (Hominy Stew)

This updated version of the traditionally long-simmered Mexican stew can be made in under half an hour, but it packs a huge punch of savory chile flavor. Canned hominy and quickly sautéed vegetables are bathed in a savory broth of ground New Mexico chiles and spices. The key ingredient is hominy, a type of maize that's soaked in an alkali solution and then dried.

YiELD 6 TO 8 CUPS   SERViNG 1½ TO 2 CUPS   PREP 10 MiNS   COOK 20 MiNS

1   In a large soup pot over medium-high heat, heat olive oil. Add yellow onion, and cook, stirring frequently and adjusting heat as necessary, for 5 minutes.

2   Stir in carrots and cremini mushrooms, and cook for 5 minutes.

3   Add garlic, and stir for 1 minute.

4   Sprinkle New Mexico chile powder, cumin, kosher salt, and oregano over vegetable mixture, and stir for 30 seconds.

5   Add vegetable stock, bring to a simmer, and cook for 5 minutes.

6   Add hominy and zucchini, bring to a boil, reduce heat to medium-low, and cook for 10 minutes.

7   Remove from heat, stir in lime juice and cilantro, and serve.

iNGREDiENTS

3 TB. olive oil

1 large yellow onion, finely chopped (about 1½ cups)

2 medium carrots, cut into ¼-in. (.5cm) rounds

1 (8-oz.; 225g) pkg. cremini (baby bella) mushrooms, thinly sliced

2 cloves garlic, finely chopped

3 TB. dried ground New Mexico chile powder

1 tsp. ground cumin

1 tsp. kosher salt

½ tsp. dried oregano

4 cups vegetable stock

1 (15-oz.; 420g) can hominy, rinsed and drained

1 medium zucchini, trimmed, quartered lengthwise, and cut into ½-inch (1.25cm) chunks

Juice of 1 medium lime (1 TB.)

2 TB. finely chopped fresh cilantro

Posole is traditionally served for special occasions. Putting little bowls on the table with different garnishes and letting guests fix their own bowls is a fun way to make this party dish really festive. Try thinly sliced radishes, jalapeños, and scallions; shredded cabbage or romaine lettuce; sliced avocado; lime wedges; plant-based sour cream; hot sauce; and tortilla chips or tostadas.

Salads

Delight in the unexpected flavors and textures of the salads in this section. Choose a hearty main-dish salad or something lighter to get things started.

Wilted Spinach Salad

Baby spinach is quickly wilted in a flavorful dressing of shiitake mushrooms accented with walnuts, Dijon mustard, and tangy apple cider vinegar.

YIELD 6 CUPS   SERVING 2 CUPS   PREP 5 MINS   COOK 10 MINS

1   In a medium sauté pan over medium-high heat, heat sesame oil. Add shiitake mushrooms, and stir for 2 minutes.

2   Add walnuts and garlic, and stir for 2 minutes. Adjust heat as needed.

3   Add red onion, kosher salt, whole-grain Dijon mustard, and apple cider vinegar, and bring to a boil. Remove from heat.

4   Slowly stir in extra-virgin olive oil. Add baby spinach, toss with hot dressing until wilted, season with black pepper, and serve.

For a *Dinner Salad*, choose a hearty green such as baby kale; add some cooked quinoa; steamed vegetables or chopped, raw veggies; and a can of rinsed and drained beans; serve with Romesco Sauce.

INGREDIENTS

1 TB. sesame oil

1 (4-oz.; 110g) pkg. shiitake mushrooms, stemmed and thinly sliced

1 cup walnuts, finely chopped

1 clove garlic, finely chopped

1 small red onion, halved and thinly sliced

½ tsp. kosher salt

1 TB. whole-grain Dijon mustard

¼ cup apple cider vinegar

½ cup extra-virgin olive oil

12 cups baby spinach, washed and spun dry

½ tsp. freshly ground black pepper

Celery Root Remoulade

Celery root, or celeriac, is grated and tossed in remoulade sauce for a quick, healthy, and delicious no-cook salad. Serve it over crisp leaf lettuce or watercress, or spread on toast for an open-faced sandwich.

YIELD 2 ½ CUP   SERVING ¼ CUP   PREP 10 MINS   COOK NONE

1   In a large bowl, whisk together mayo, extra-virgin olive oil, Dijon mustard, lemon juice, cornichon pickles, grated onion, Italian flat-leaf parsley, kosher salt, and black pepper. Set aside.

2   Wash and peel celery root, and quarter it. Working quickly, grate each quarter into the bowl with remoulade sauce. Toss and serve over lettuce leaves immediately. Once made, this dish will keep in the refrigerator for up to 2 days.

INGREDIENTS

¼ cup plus 1 TB. plant-based mayo

2 TB. extra-virgin olive oil

2 TB. Dijon mustard

Juice of 1 medium lemon (2 TB.)

2 TB. finely chopped cornichon pickles

1 TB. finely grated onion

1 TB. finely chopped fresh Italian flat-leaf parsley

½ tsp. kosher salt

½ tsp. freshly ground black pepper

1 (1½ lb.; 680g) celery root

Lettuce leaves or toast

GREENS

Delicious and nutrient-packed greens include kale, spinach, collards, and chard. Their flavors pair well with cheese, garlic, onions, potatoes, olive oil, avocados, mushrooms, lemons, nutmeg, curry, and chiles. **Benefits** Strengthen bones, anti-inflammatory, lower cholesterol, reduce cancer risk. **Uses** Kale is in season in autumn and winter, spinach is good late spring to autumn, and chard is at its peak in early summer and early autumn. Eat fresh during these times in salads or cooked in soups and stews. **Recipes** Ginger Kale Soup; Wilted Spinach Salad; Spinach and Rice–Stuffed Tomatoes; Creamy Pasta with Swiss Chard and Roasted Tomatoes; Swiss Chard Ravioli.

Roasted Beet Salad

Sweet beets combine with the bright flavors of citrus and toasty walnuts for a delicious and very fancy-looking salad that's perfect for a celebration meal or dinner party.

YIELD 6 CUPS   SERVING 1½ CUPS   PREP 10 MINS   COOK 30 MINS

1   Preheat the oven to 400°F (200°C).

2   Scrub beets but do not peel. Place beets in a baking dish, drizzle with 1 tablespoon extra-virgin olive oil, and roast for 30 to 40 minutes or until easily pierced with a fork. Remove from the oven, and set aside to cool.

3   Reduce oven temperature to 350°F (180°C).

4   Spread walnuts in a single layer on a baking sheet, and toast for 7 minutes or until golden, stirring once. Cool slightly, and chop coarsely.

5   After using a Microplane grater to remove zest from 1 orange, segment oranges. Using a sharp paring knife, cut about ¼ inch (.5cm) from the top and bottom of the fruit, and carefully cut away peel and pith. You should see the membrane that separates each segment. Place orange flat, cut side down on a rimmed cutting board, and very carefully use your paring knife to cut along the inside of each segment, slicing as close to membrane as possible. A neat supreme of orange will pop out. Place supremes in a separate bowl, and repeat with remaining segments, stopping occasionally to pour juice on the board into a bowl.

6   In the bowl with reserved orange juice, whisk together orange zest, shallot, lemon juice, Dijon mustard, kosher salt, and black pepper. Slowly drizzle in remaining ¼ cup extra-virgin olive oil, whisking constantly.

7   Peel beets, cut into ½-inch (1.25cm) wedges, and toss with ½ of vinaigrette and orange segments.

8   Arrange 1 cup mesclun greens on each of 4 plates, drizzle with remaining dressing, and evenly divide beet mixture over greens. Sprinkle each salad with ¼ of walnuts, and serve.

INGREDIENTS

4 large beets

1 TB. plus ¼ cup extra-virgin olive oil

1 cup walnut halves

Zest of 1 medium orange (1 TB.)

2 medium seedless navel oranges

1 shallot, finely minced

Juice of 1 lemon (2 TB.)

1 tsp. Dijon mustard

1 tsp. kosher salt

½ tsp. freshly ground black pepper

4 cups mesclun greens or torn lettuce

The beet mixture can be prepared up to 3 days in advance. When ready to serve, toast walnuts and plate as directed.

Roasted Tomato and White Bean Salad

Plum tomatoes are roasted until sweet and tossed with cannellini beans, red onion, and arugula for a healthy and flavorful salad.

YIELD 6 CUPS   SERVING 1½ CUPS   PREP 10 MINS   COOK 40 MINS

1 Preheat the oven to 350°F (180°C).

2 Place plum tomato halves on a rimmed baking sheet, cut side up, and tuck 1 or 2 slices of garlic into each piece. Drizzle with 1 tablespoon olive oil, and season with kosher salt and black pepper. Roast for 40 minutes, and cool slightly.

3 In a medium bowl, toss cannellini beans with remaining 2 tablespoons olive oil, red onion, and arugula.

4 Divide salad among 4 chilled plates, spoon roasted tomatoes and any juices remaining in the pan over salad, and serve immediately.

INGREDIENTS

12 plum tomatoes, cored and halved lengthwise

2 cloves garlic, cut in very thin slices

3 TB. olive oil

1 tsp. kosher salt

½ tsp. freshly ground black pepper

1 (14-oz.; 400g) can cannellini beans, rinsed and drained

½ small red onion, very thinly sliced

1 bunch arugula, tough stems removed, washed, spun dry, and chilled

Plum tomatoes

For *White Bean and Red Pepper Salad,* use slices of jarred roasted red peppers instead of tomatoes.

Picnic Potato Salad Ⓣ

Tender new potatoes are bathed in a sauce of mayo, herbs, and lots of crunchy celery and dill pickles in this perfect potato salad.

YIELD 7 CUPS   **SERVING** ½ CUP   **PREP** 10 MINS   **COOK** 15 MINS PLUS COOL TIME

1. In a pot with a tight-fitting lid, bring 2 inches (5cm) water to a boil over medium-high heat. Place new potatoes in a steamer basket, set in the pot, and steam for about 10 minutes or until tender and easily pierced with a fork. Transfer to a wide colander to drain and cool for 15 minutes.

2. Meanwhile, in a large bowl, whisk together mayo, extra-virgin olive oil, whole-grain Dijon mustard, apple cider vinegar, dill, Italian flat-leaf parsley, hot sauce, kosher salt, and black pepper until smooth and well combined. Reserve ½ of dressing in a small bowl.

3. When potatoes are cool enough to handle, cut in halves or quarters.

4. Fold red onion, celery, and dill pickle into sauce in the large bowl, and gently fold in potatoes. Refrigerate along with reserved dressing for 1 hour or until chilled.

5. Fold in reserved dressing, and serve. Potato salad will keep in the refrigerator for up to 3 days.

INGREDIENTS

3 lb. (1.5kg) small new (red) potatoes

¾ cup plant-based mayo

¼ cup extra-virgin olive oil

2 TB. whole-grain Dijon mustard

2 TB. apple cider vinegar

2 TB. finely chopped fresh dill

2 TB. finely chopped fresh Italian flat-leaf parsley

1 tsp. hot sauce, such as Crystal or Tabasco

1½ tsp. kosher salt

½ tsp. freshly ground black pepper

1 medium red onion, finely chopped

4 medium stalks celery, finely chopped (1½ cups)

½ cup finely chopped dill pickle

Waxy potatoes make the best potato salad. Floury potatoes such as russet absorb too much dressing and fall apart, resulting in a salad with a mashed-potato consistency. I like the extra nutrition of unpeeled potatoes, but if you prefer a potato salad with peeled potatoes, substitute larger white or yellow potatoes. Steam in their skins, cool, and peel.

Insalata Rinforzo (Neapolitan Christmas Salad)

This traditional Neapolitan Christmas salad features tender cauliflower that's taken to flavorful perfection with briny olives and capers and just the right amount of vinegar. *Rinforzo* means "reinforcement," as this salad is traditionally made for Christmas Eve and then replenished throughout the days of the Christmas season.

YiELD 6 CUPS   SERViNG 1 CUP   PREP 10 MiNS   COOK 20 MiNS

1   In a pot with a tight-fitting lid, bring 1 inch (2.5cm) water to a boil over medium-high heat. Place cauliflower in a steamer basket, set in the pot, and steam for about 6 minutes or until tender. Remove cauliflower to a large bowl, and immediately toss with garlic and red onion.

2   Using a silicone spatula, gently stir in roasted red bell peppers, Gaeta olives, Cerignola olives, and capers. Drizzle with extra-virgin olive oil, and toss gently.

3   Add red wine vinegar, Italian flat-leaf parsley, and black pepper, and toss again. Taste and add more vinegar or black pepper if desired. Serve immediately, or refrigerate for up to 1 week.

INGREDiENTS

1 medium head cauliflower, broken into small florets

1 clove garlic, finely chopped, plus more to taste

½ small red onion, sliced paper thin

4 roasted red bell peppers, thinly sliced

1 cup pitted black Gaeta olives

1 cup pitted green Cerignola olives

¼ cup salted capers, rinsed and drained

½ cup extra-virgin olive oil

¼ cup red wine vinegar, or to taste

¼ cup finely chopped fresh Italian flat-leaf parsley

½ tsp. freshly ground black pepper, plus more to taste

Tossing the hot cauliflower with the onion and garlic cooks and softens the garlic and onion, tempering their flavor. You can vary the amount of garlic to your liking, too. To "reinforce" the salad, steam some more cauliflower; add more olives, peppers, and whatever else you like; and drizzle with more oil and vinegar. If you can't find Gaeta or Cerignola olives, substitute any flavorful olives you like. Oil-cured black olives are another great choice.

Warm Fingerling Potato Salad with Grainy Mustard Vinaigrette

Flavorful fingerling potatoes are dressed quite simply, with plenty of shallots and grainy mustard, and spooned over a bed of leafy greens.

YiELD 4 CUPS   **SERViNG** 1 CUP   **PREP** 5 MiNS   **COOK** 10 MiNS

1   In a pot with a tight-fitting lid, bring 1 inch (2.5cm) water to a boil. Place fingerling potatoes in a steamer basket, set in the pot, and steam for about 8 to 10 minutes or until tender and easily pierced with a fork. Transfer potatoes to a large bowl.

2   While potatoes are steaming, in a small bowl, whisk together shallots, whole-grain Dijon mustard, sherry vinegar, and kosher salt. Slowly whisk in extra-virgin olive oil in a thin stream, and whisk in chervil, chives, Italian flat-leaf parsley, and black pepper.

3   Reserve ¼ cup dressing, and toss potatoes with remainder of dressing.

4   Divide mesclun salad greens among 4 chilled plates, spoon ¼ of potato salad over greens, and drizzle each serving with 1 tablespoon reserved dressing. Serve immediately.

INGREDIENTS

1 lb. (450g) small fingerling potatoes, halved lengthwise

1 medium shallot, halved and very thinly sliced

2 TB. whole-grain Dijon mustard

¼ cup sherry vinegar

1 tsp. kosher salt

½ cup extra-virgin olive oil

2 TB. finely chopped fresh chervil

2 TB. finely chopped fresh chives

2 TB. finely chopped fresh Italian flat-leaf parsley

½ tsp. freshly ground black pepper

8 cups mesclun salad greens or baby spinach, washed, spun dry, and chilled

Shallot

For *Warm Potato Salad Supper,* add 1 (14-ounce; 400g) can cannellini beans, rinsed and drained, and 2 cups halved cherry or grape tomatoes.

Warm Lentil, Barley, and Sweet Potato Salad (T)

Warm lentils, barley, and roasted sweet potatoes are tossed in a pomegranate and Dijon mustard dressing, then sprinkled with bright, nutrient-packed pomegranate seeds for a flavorful, filling, and nutritious "main dish" salad.

YiELD 5 OR 6 CUPS   **SERVING** 1¼ CUPS   **PREP** 10 MINS   **COOK** 40 MINS

1 In a medium saucepan with a lid, combine green lentils, pearl barley, garlic, and bay leaf. Add water to cover by 2 inches (5cm). Bring to a boil, reduce heat to medium-low, and cook for 40 minutes or until tender. Drain, remove and discard bay leaf, and cool slightly.

2 Meanwhile, preheat the oven to 400°F (200°C).

3 On a baking sheet lined with parchment paper, toss sweet potato with 1 tablespoon extra-virgin olive oil. Roast, stirring once, for 30 minutes. Cool slightly.

4 In a small bowl, whisk together lemon juice, shallot, pomegranate molasses, Dijon mustard, kosher salt, and black pepper until well combined. Slowly drizzle in remaining 2 tablespoons extra-virgin olive oil, whisking continuously.

5 In a wide serving bowl, gently fold together lentils, barley, and sweet potatoes. Toss with ¾ of dressing. Sprinkle with pomegranate seeds, drizzle with remaining dressing, and serve warm.

INGREDIENTS

½ cup small green (du Puy) lentils

½ cup pearl barley

1 clove garlic, lightly smashed

1 bay leaf

1 large sweet potato, peeled and cut in 1-in. (2.5cm) dice

3 TB. extra-virgin olive oil

Juice of 1 lemon (2 TB.)

1 small shallot, finely chopped

1 TB. pomegranate molasses

1 TB. Dijon mustard

½ tsp. kosher salt

¼ tsp. freshly ground black pepper

Seeds from 1 pomegranate

Pomegranate molasses is sold in Middle Eastern grocery stores. If you can't find it locally, order a bottle online. It's a fantastic addition to eggplant stew, salad dressings, and anything that needs a sweet—but not too sweet—flavor enhancement. Speaking of pomegranates, everyone has a favorite way of seeding one. A quick internet search should yield plenty of instructional videos if you need help.

Herbed Tabbouleh

Tabbouleh is a wonderful Middle Eastern dish of bulgur wheat, tomatoes, onions, and plenty of parsley. Serve it with hummus, lentil soup, and some warm pita for a wonderful, soul-satisfying meal, or simply enjoy it for lunch with crisp spears of romaine lettuce for scooping.

YIELD 6 CUPS   SERVING 1 CUP   PREP 15 MINS   COOK NONE

1   Rinse bulgur wheat. Add to a medium bowl with 1 tablespoon extra-virgin olive oil, pour near-boiling water over top, and stir. Let stand for 15 minutes and then strain in a fine-mesh sieve, pressing gently to remove all liquid. Fluff with a fork.

2   In a large bowl, toss bulgur with curly parsley, mint, scallions, tomatoes, English cucumber, red onion, lemon juice, remaining 3 tablespoons extra-virgin olive oil, kosher salt, and black pepper. Cover, and set aside to allow flavors to blend for 1 hour.

3   Serve at room temperature or cold. Tabbouleh will keep in the refrigerator for 3 days.

INGREDIENTS

½ cup fine bulgur wheat

4 TB. extra-virgin olive oil

1 cup near-boiling water

3 bunches fresh curly parsley, stems removed, finely chopped (4 to 4½ cups)

¼ cup finely chopped fresh mint

4 scallions, thinly sliced

2 large tomatoes, cored, seeded, and finely chopped

½ English cucumber, peeled, seeded, and finely chopped

½ small red onion, finely chopped (¼ cup)

Juice of 2 medium lemons (¼ cup)

1 tsp. kosher salt

½ tsp. freshly ground black pepper

Tabbouleh is traditionally made with curly parsley. Italian flat-leaf parsley won't provide the same slightly chewy consistency or intensity of flavor.

Vegetables

Eating plant based means you don't have to think about what will fill the center of your plate—vegetables! Serve several veggie dishes together for an unforgettable meal.

Imam Bayildi (Turkish Stuffed Eggplant)

When eggplant is in season, try this delicious dish. The olive oil, onions, tomatoes, and garlic are the perfect complement to meaty eggplant. Soak up the delicious juices with pita bread or rice.

YiELD 6 STUFFED EGGPLANTS   SERViNG 1 EGGPLANT   PREP 10 MiNS PLUS 1 HOUR SOAK TiME   COOK 60 MiNS

1 Fill the kitchen sink or a large tub with well-salted water. Cut a small slit in each eggplant, add to salt water bath, and soak for 1 hour. Drain, squeeze gently, and pat dry.

2 In a wide, ovenproof sauté pan or a Dutch oven with a lid over medium heat, heat extra-virgin olive oil. Add sweet onions, and cook, stirring occasionally, for about 5 to 10 minutes or until golden.

3 Add eggplants, plum tomatoes, and garlic, reduce heat to medium-low (adjust as needed), cover, and cook, stirring onions once or twice without disturbing eggplants, for 10 minutes.

4 Turn eggplants, and cook for 10 minutes.

5 Preheat the oven to 375°F (190°C).

6 Remove the sauté pan from heat, and gently stuff some onion-tomato mixture into each eggplant. Pour reserved tomato juice over eggplants, sprinkle with Italian flat-leaf parsley, cover tightly with a lid or foil, and bake for 35 to 40 minutes.

7 Remove from the oven, and cool slightly before garnishing with toasted pine nuts (if using) and serving.

INGREDiENTS

6 small eggplants, stems removed

½ cup extra-virgin olive oil, plus more to taste

3 large sweet onions, halved and thinly sliced

6 ripe plum tomatoes, peeled, julienne cut, and juice reserved

6 cloves garlic, thinly sliced

¼ cup fresh Italian flat-leaf parsley, finely chopped, plus more for garnish

¼ cup toasted pine nuts (optional)

Red Cabbage with Apples and Pecans

Lightly pickled red onions pair perfectly with just-cooked red cabbage and apple with a toasty pecan topping. The gorgeous red colors of this dish make it a perfect choice to brighten your holiday table.

YIELD 4 CUPS   **SERVING** ½ CUP   **PREP** 15 TO 20 MINS   **COOK** 15 MINS

1 In a large nonstick sauté pan or wide, large saucepan over medium-high heat, heat extra-virgin olive oil. Add red onion and kosher salt, and cook, stirring frequently, for 4 or 5 minutes or until onion is limp.

2 Reduce heat to medium, and remove the pan from the burner for about 30 seconds.

3 Stir in apple cider vinegar and whole-grain Dijon mustard, and stir to and coat onions.

4 Return the pan to the burner, and cook for 30 seconds to 1 minute to reduce slightly if needed.

5 Stir in apple and red cabbage. If mixture looks dry, add 1 tablespoon water. Cover, reduce heat to medium, and cook for 5 minutes, stirring once or twice and adding more water as needed.

6 Uncover, stir, and continue to cook until cabbage is crisp-tender.

7 Season with black pepper, and sprinkle with pecans. Serve hot, warm, or cold.

INGREDIENTS

2 TB. extra-virgin olive oil

1 large red onion, halved and thinly sliced (1½ cups)

1 tsp. kosher salt

¼ cup apple cider vinegar

1 tsp. whole-grain Dijon mustard

1 large, crisp apple, such as Fuji, skin on, cored, and thinly sliced

1 small red cabbage, cored, quartered, and thinly sliced (about 5 cups)

1 or 2 TB. water

½ tsp. freshly ground black pepper

½ cup toasted, chopped pecans

To make *Toasted Nuts*, preheat the oven to 350°F (180°C). Spread pecans or your favorite nuts on a baking sheet lined with parchment paper and bake, stirring once or twice, for 6 or 7 minutes or until nuts are fragrant and toasty. I like to roast a big batch and store them in a tightly sealed glass jar at room temperature until needed. They'll keep for weeks this way, and it saves time to have them toasted and ready to go to add quick crunch and flavor to a finished dish or baked item.

Stir-Fried Chinese Cress with Fermented Black Beans

The bitter flavor of Chinese watercress is a perfect foil to the deeply umami flavor of fermented black beans (available bagged at your local Asian grocery store) and a kick of garlic.

YiELD 6 CUPS **SERViNG** 1½ CUPS **PREP** 5 MiNS **COOK** 5 MiNS

1   Heat a wok or large cast-iron skillet over medium heat until hot. Add grapeseed oil, garlic, and ginger, and stir for 30 seconds.

2   Add Chinese watercress, and stir for 30 seconds.

3   Stir in vegetable stock, fermented black beans, and crushed red pepper flakes. Stir for 1 or 2 more minutes or until beans are heated through and cress is tender, and serve immediately.

INGREDIENTS

2 TB. grapeseed oil

8 cloves garlic, very thinly sliced

1 TB. grated fresh ginger

4 bunches Chinese watercress, washed well, bottom 1 in. (2.5cm) of stem removed (about 12 cups)

¼ cup vegetable stock

½ cup fermented black beans

½ tsp. crushed red pepper flakes

For *Quick and Easy Stir-Fry*—and dinner on the table in under 15 minutes—serve this over cooked rice noodles.

Roasted Tomatoes

Small tomatoes become sweet, with a concentrated tomato flavor, when roasted slowly with garlic, salt, and olive oil. Toss them with pasta, pile on a sandwich, stir into salads, use them as a base for savory sauces, or just eat them with a spoon!

YiELD 4 CUPS **SERVING** 1 CUP **PREP** 20 MINS **COOK** 1 HOUR

1 Preheat the oven to 300°F (150°C). Arrange two racks in the lower third of the oven.

2 Divide cherry tomatoes, cut side up, between 2 rimmed baking sheets. Insert 1 garlic slice into each half, drizzle with olive oil, and season lightly with kosher salt and black pepper.

3 Bake for about 1 hour, stirring once or twice, or until tomatoes are reduced and very soft. Serve warm or at room temperature. Leftovers will keep in the refrigerator for up to 3 days.

INGREDiENTS

2 lb. (1kg) cherry tomatoes, halved

3 cloves garlic, sliced very thin

2 TB. olive oil

1 tsp. kosher salt

½ tsp. freshly ground black pepper

Cherry tomatoes

For *Tomato Basil Pasta Salad*, toss a batch of these tomatoes with 1 pound (450g) penne, cooked according to package directions, drained, and rinsed with cold water. Stir in 1 cup lightly packed torn fresh basil leaves and ½ cup pitted Niçoise olives, and serve.

Herbed Zucchini

Tender slices of zucchini are brushed with plant-based mayo and encrusted with panko, fresh herbs, and olive oil for a lower-fat version of a fried favorite. Serve plain or with tomato sauce.

YIELD 24 SLICES   SERVING 6 SLICES   PREP 10 MINS   COOK 20 MINS

1   Preheat the oven to 400°F (200°C). Line a baking sheet with parchment paper.

2   Trim each zucchini, cut into ¼-inch (.5cm) slices. Blot dry with paper towels, and brush both sides of each zucchini slice with mayonnaise.

3   In a small, shallow bowl, combine panko, herbs, extra-virgin olive oil, kosher salt, black pepper, and lemon zest.

4   Dredge each zucchini slice in panko mixture, coating both sides, and lay slices on the prepared baking sheet.

5   Bake for 20 minutes, carefully turning with a spatula halfway through cooking, and serve immediately.

INGREDIENTS

2 large (about 8-in.; 20cm) zucchini

¼ cup plant-based mayonnaise

2 cups panko breadcrumbs

½ cup finely chopped fresh mixed herbs such as parsley, chives, chervil, and/or tarragon

½ cup extra-virgin olive oil

2 tsp. kosher salt

1 tsp. freshly ground black pepper

2 tsp. lemon zest

Sautéed Broccoli Rabe

Broccoli rabe is a slightly bitter cruciferous vegetable that's incredibly flavorful when prepared with garlic and olive oil. Try this dish as a side, spread on a sandwich, added to cooked beans, or served with pasta.

YIELD 4 CUPS **SERVING** 1 CUP **PREP** 5 MINS **COOK** 10 MINS

1 Wash broccoli rabe, and trim off tough bottom end of each stem (about ½ inch; 1.25cm).

2 In a medium saucepan over high heat, bring enough water to cover broccoli rabe by 1 inch (2.5cm) to a boil. Add ½ teaspoon kosher salt and broccoli rabe, blanch for 1 minute, transfer to an ice bath to cool quickly, drain, and set aside.

3 In a medium sauté pan over medium heat, heat extra-virgin olive oil and garlic. When garlic begins to sizzle and turn a golden color (but before it browns), add broccoli rabe, toss to combine, and cook, stirring frequently, for 5 minutes or until broccoli rabe is tender.

4 Season with remaining 1 teaspoon kosher salt and crushed red pepper flakes, and serve immediately.

INGREDIENTS

1 large bunch broccoli rabe, about 1 lb. (450g)

1 tsp. kosher salt

2 TB. extra-virgin olive oil

3 cloves garlic, thinly sliced

½ tsp. crushed red pepper flakes

Southern-Style Braised Greens

Nutritious greens are slowly braised until tender in flavorful vegetable stock seasoned with olive oil, garlic, onions, and a little smoked sea salt. Add some beans and fresh bread for a dinner dish.

YIELD 6 CUPS **SERVING** 1 OR 2 CUPS **PREP** 15 MINS **COOK** 35 MINS

1 In a large saucepan or soup pot over high heat, combine vegetable stock, extra-virgin olive oil, smoked sea salt, black pepper, and garlic. Bring to a boil.

2 Stir in collard greens, mustard greens, and curly kale. Reduce heat to medium, and cook, uncovered and stirring occasionally, for about 35 minutes or until greens are tender. Adjust heat to maintain a gentle simmer.

3 Season greens with apple cider vinegar, and serve with a little of the liquid that remains in the pot (pot liquor).

INGREDIENTS

4 cups vegetable stock

¼ cup extra-virgin olive oil

1 tsp. smoked sea salt

½ tsp. freshly ground black pepper

2 cloves garlic, crushed and finely chopped

1 large bunch collard greens, tough stems removed, cut in small pieces

1 large bunch mustard greens, tough stems removed, cut in small pieces

1 large bunch curly kale, tough stems removed, cut in small pieces

1 TB. apple cider vinegar, or juice of ½ lemon (1 TB.)

CRUCIFEROUS VEGETABLES

Cruciferous vegetables such as broccoli, cauliflower, and cabbage are loaded with vitamin A carotenoids, vitamin C, folic acid, and fiber. They're easily adaptable to fit a wide variety of dishes. **Benefits** Lower cancer risk, support liver function, improve skin health, aid eye health, boost immunity. **Uses** Choose firm and brightly colored vegetables with moist ends, and eat raw in salads and wraps, or boil, steam, stir-fry, sauté, bake, or braise. **Recipes** Sesame Ginger Broccoli, Curried Cauliflower Coconut Soup, Mushroom and Cabbage Borscht, Red Cabbage with Apples and Pecans, Savory Stuffed Cabbage, *Insalata Rinforzo*, Minestrone.

Spinach and Rice–Stuffed Tomatoes

When juicy beefsteak tomatoes are in season, buy the largest ones you can find and stuff them with cheesy rice, spinach, and pine nuts. Bake until tender and sweet for an irresistible taste of summer.

YIELD 6 TOMATOES   SERVING 1 TOMATO   PREP 20 MINS   COOK 60 MINS

1. Preheat the oven to 400°F (200°C). Lightly grease a baking dish large enough to hold tomatoes snugly.

2. In a small saucepan over medium-high heat, bring water to a boil. Add Arborio rice and ½ teaspoon kosher salt, and cook for exactly 10 minutes. Remove from heat, drain, and set aside.

3. Working over a colander set over a large bowl, core beefsteak tomatoes and scoop out insides, removing seeds and pulp while leaving outer flesh and skin intact. Press gently on pulp to remove as much liquid as possible. Place hollowed tomatoes in baking dish, and set juice aside.

4. In a wide sauté pan over medium heat, heat olive oil. Add red onion, season with ¼ teaspoon kosher salt, and cook, stirring frequently, for about 5 to 7 minutes or until soft and beginning to color.

5. Add garlic, and cook for 1 minute.

6. Increase heat to high, add spinach, and cook for about 3 minutes or until wilted.

7. In a large bowl, combine rice, spinach, mozzarella-style cheese, toasted pine nuts, nutritional yeast, Italian flat-leaf parsley, basil, nutmeg, black pepper, and remaining ¾ teaspoon salt.

8. Spoon rice mixture into tomatoes, filling each to the top. Pour tomato juice over and around stuffed tomatoes, cover pan tightly with aluminum foil, and bake for 25 minutes or until hot and bubbling.

9. Uncover, and cook 5 more minutes. Drizzle with lemon juice, and serve hot or warm.

INGREDIENTS

2¾ cups water

¾ cup Arborio rice

1½ tsp. kosher salt

6 large beefsteak tomatoes

3 TB. olive oil

1 medium red onion, finely chopped (1 cup)

2 cloves garlic, thinly sliced

1 lb. (450g) spinach, washed in several changes of cold water, shaken dry in a colander, thick stems removed, thinly sliced

1 cup shredded plant-based mozzarella-style cheese, preferably almond based

½ cup toasted pine nuts

¼ cup nutritional yeast

2 TB. finely chopped fresh Italian flat-leaf parsley leaves

2 TB. torn or sliced fresh basil leaves

¼ tsp. freshly ground nutmeg

¼ tsp. freshly ground black pepper

Juice of 1 lemon (2 TB.)

Fried Green Tomatoes

Unripe green tomatoes are dredged in cornmeal and quickly fried for a delicious classic born of the desire not to waste food. Make these in autumn, before the first frost, with the last tomatoes on the vine—or cheat and sneak some in early summer before they ripen!

YiELD 20 SLiCES   **SERViNG** 4 OR 5 SLiCES   **PREP** 5 MiNS   **COOK** 10 MiNS

1 Core each beefsteak tomato, trim and discard ⅛ inch (3mm) from the top and bottom, and cut into 5 even slices. Set aside.

2 In a medium bowl, whisk together soy milk and lemon juice. Set aside to curdle for a few minutes.

3 Place cornmeal on a rimmed plate.

4 In a large frying pan over medium-high heat, heat ½ inch (1.25cm) grapeseed oil until it's shimmering.

5 Working with just enough tomato slices to fit comfortably in the pan, dip each tomato slice in soy milk mixture and dredge in cornmeal. Add to the pan, fry for about 2 minutes, adjusting heat as necessary to prevent burning. Turn carefully with a spatula, and fry other side for 2 more minutes. Transfer to a plate lined with several thicknesses of paper towels, season with a little kosher salt and black pepper, and keep warm. Continue until all tomato slices have been fried, replacing oil if cornmeal begins to burn. Serve hot.

INGREDiENTS

4 large, green beefsteak tomatoes

½ cup unsweetened soy milk

Juice of ½ lemon (1 TB.)

1¼ cups fine cornmeal

Grapeseed oil

½ tsp. kosher salt

½ tsp. freshly ground black pepper

Kosher salt

For a *Fried Green Tomato Sandwich,* pile fried tomato slices on a crusty roll spread with a little plant-based mayo, hot sauce, and crispy lettuce.

Stuffed Artichokes Ⓣ

This Italian American classic is a fantastic holiday appetizer, but it also makes a wonderful supper with a cup of soup and a simple salad. Artichokes are easier to prepare than you might think, and they are simply delicious when stuffed with a flavorful breadcrumb mixture bursting with the briny flavors of capers, olives, and plenty of garlic.

YIELD 4 ARTICHOKES   **SERVING** 1 ARTICHOKE   **PREP** 25 MINS   **COOK** 50 MINS

1 Preheat the oven to 375°F (190°C). Lightly grease a baking dish large enough to hold artichokes.

2 Clean and prep artichokes.

3 In a small sauté pan over medium heat, heat extra-virgin olive oil. Add Spanish olives, capers, and garlic, and cook, stirring frequently, for 3 minutes or until garlic just begins to color. Remove from heat.

4 In a medium bowl, combine Italian-seasoned breadcrumbs, Italian flat-leaf parsley, lemon zest, black pepper, and olive oil mixture.

5 Pat artichokes dry. Spread apart leaves of 1 artichoke, and spoon ¼ of breadcrumb mixture between leaves and into center of artichoke. Repeat with remaining artichokes, nestling them snugly in the baking dish after stuffing.

6 Pour 1 inch (2.5cm) boiling water around artichokes, taking care not to pour water directly over them (this will result in soggy filling). Lightly grease a piece of aluminum foil, and cover the pan tightly.

7 Bake for 45 minutes, uncover, and bake for 5 more minutes. Serve hot or at room temperature.

INGREDIENTS

4 large globe artichokes

½ cup extra-virgin olive oil

¼ cup green Spanish (Manzanilla) olives, finely chopped

1 TB. salted capers, rinsed, drained, and finely chopped

6 cloves garlic, minced

1½ cups Italian-seasoned breadcrumbs

¼ cup finely chopped fresh Italian flat-leaf parsley

1 tsp. grated lemon zest

½ tsp. freshly ground black pepper

Boiling water

To prepare artichokes for cooking, cut off the bottom part of the stem and the top ¼ inch (.5cm) of leaves, and snap off the first few layers of tough, dark green outer leaves. With a sharp pair of kitchen scissors, cut the sharp edges off the top of each remaining leaf. Spread out the artichoke leaves from the center, and use a sharp grapefruit spoon to scrape out the spiny, purple "choke" from the center, leaving the heart intact. Rub the artichokes with a cut lemon as you work, and place each cleaned artichoke into a bath of cold water with a few tablespoons lemon juice to keep them from turning brown.

Almond and Breadcrumb–Stuffed Piquillo Peppers

Tangy piquillo peppers are stuffed with a savory almond and breadcrumb filling. Pass them on a tray at your next party, and they'll quickly disappear.

YiELD 14 PEPPERS   SERViNG 2 PEPPERS   PREP 10 MiNS   COOK 30 MiNS

1   Preheat the oven to 350°F (180°C).

2   In a small saucepan over medium-high heat, heat 1 tablespoon extra-virgin olive oil. Add garlic, shallot, and crushed red pepper flakes, and cook for 30 seconds. Stir in Italian flat-leaf parsley, and remove from heat.

3   In a small bowl, combine breadcrumbs, Marcona almonds, capers, and garlic mixture. Stir in 1 tablespoon extra-virgin olive oil.

4   Drizzle a medium baking dish with half of remaining extra-virgin olive oil (about 1 teaspoon). Gently fill each piquillo pepper with about 1 tablespoon stuffing, and place filled peppers in the baking dish. Drizzle stuffed peppers with remaining extra-virgin olive oil, and bake for 20 minutes. Serve hot, warm, or at room temperature.

INGREDIENTS

3 TB. extra-virgin olive oil

2 cloves garlic, finely chopped

1 small shallot, finely chopped

½ tsp. crushed red pepper flakes

2 TB. finely chopped fresh Italian flat-leaf parsley

1 cup fresh breadcrumbs

½ cup finely chopped Marcona almonds

1 TB. salted capers, rinsed, drained, and finely chopped

1 (14-oz.; 400g) can piquillo peppers, drained

Piquillo peppers are small, pointed, slightly spicy peppers from Spain. If you don't have a well-stocked Spanish grocery nearby, you can find them online. If you absolutely can't get them, you can use Peppadew peppers instead.

Vegetables

Vegetables are a fresh and delicious way to get protein, fiber, vitamins, and minerals. Eating a rainbow of colorful vegetables each day provides disease-fighting antioxidants and micronutrients. Raw and cooked vegetables form the bulk of a healthy plant-based diet, so choose a wide variety daily to reap the greatest nutritional benefit.

Carrots

	ARTICHOKES	ASPARAGUS	AVOCADOS	BROCCOLI	BROCCOLI RABE	BRUSSEL SPROUTS	CARROTS	CAULIFLOWER
USES	Scoop out choke, trim ends of leaves, rub with lemon, and steam, stuff, or use prepared artichoke hearts in salads, dips, and casseroles.	Steam, roast, grill, or blanch. Use in soups, salads, casseroles, and pasta dishes.	Halve, pit, and scoop out creamy flesh. Slice or cube for salads, stews, soups, or Mexican dishes. Spread on toast or bagels, or use in dips, salad dressings, and even desserts.	Blanch, steam, sauté, or serve raw. Use in soups, salads, casseroles, and pasta dishes.	Blanch or steam and then sauté with garlic and olive oil.	Roast, steam, sauté, or serve raw.	Aromatic; use with celery and onions to flavor soups, stews, or sauces. Roast, steam, or sauté.	Steam, blanch, roast, or serve raw. Use in salads, soups, casseroles, pasta dishes, curries, and stews.
GOOD SOURCE OF ...	Protein, fiber, vitamins C and K, niacin, magnesium, phosphorus, potassium, copper, folate, and manganese.	Protein; fiber; vitamins C, A, E, K; thiamin; riboflavin; niacin; folate; phosphorus; potassium; copper; manganese; and selenium.	Healthy fats, protein, fiber, vitamins K and C, and folate.	Protein; vitamins E, A, C, K, B_6; thiamin; riboflavin; pantothenic acid; calcium; iron; magnesium; phosphorus selenium; fiber; folate; potassium; and manganese.	Protein; fiber; vitamins A, C, E (alpha tocopherol), K, B_6; thiamin; riboflavin; niacin; folate; calcium; iron; magnesium; phosphorus; potassium; zinc; and manganese.	Fiber; thiamin; riboflavin; iron; magnesium; phosphorus; copper; vitamins A, C, K, B_6; folate; potassium; and manganese.	Fiber; thiamin; niacin; vitamins B_6, A, C, K; folate; manganese; and potassium.	Protein; fiber; thiamin; riboflavin; niacin; magnesium; phosphorus; vitamins C, K, and B_6; folate; pantothenic acid, potassium, and manganese.

Artichokes

Asparagus

Broccoli

Tomatoes

Potatoes

CORN	GREENS	KALE	MUSHROOMS	PEPPERS	POTATOES	SPINACH	SWEET POTATOES	TOMATOES
Steam, blanch, or roast. Use in soups, stews, casseroles, bean dishes, relishes, and salads.	Steam or blanch and then sauté. Use in soups, stews, and bean dishes.	Steam, blanch, sauté, or use raw. Use in soups, salads, casseroles, pasta dishes, and bean dishes.	Sauté, roast, bake and stuff, or enjoy raw. Use in salads, sautéed dishes, soups, and stews. Bread and fry for a meaty "cutlet."	Sauté or serve raw. Use as an aromatic flavor base for soups, stews, and sauces when combined with celery and onions.	Steam, bake, or roast. Use in side dishes, casseroles, soups, and stews.	Steam, blanch, sauté, or serve raw. Use in soups, stews, salads, casseroles, and curries.	Bake, roast, steam, and mash. Use in soups, stews, casseroles, salads, and side dishes.	Serve raw, roasted, or sautéed or in sauces, soups, stews, salads, dressings, chilies, and casseroles.
Protein, fiber, iron, and vitamin A.	Protein; fiber; thiamin; riboflavin; niacin; iron; magnesium; vitamins A, C, E, K, B_6; folate; calcium; phosphorus; potassium; copper; and manganese.	Protein; thiamin; riboflavin; folate; iron; magnesium; vitamins A, C, K, B_6; calcium; potassium; copper; and manganese.	Protein; fiber; vitamins C, D, B_6; folate; iron; zinc; manganese; thiamin; riboflavin; niacin; pantothenic acid; phosphorus; potassium; copper; and selenium.	Fiber; vitamins K, A, C, E (alpha tocopherol), B_6; thiamin; riboflavin; niacin; potassium; manganese; dietary fiber; folate.	Protein, fiber, vitamins C and B_6, potassium, and manganese.	Protein; fiber; niacin; zinc; vitamins A, C, E, K, B_6; thiamin; riboflavin; folate; calcium; iron; magnesium; phosphorus; potassium; copper; and manganese.	Protein; fiber; vitamins B_6, A, and C; potassium; and manganese.	Fiber; niacin; vitamins B_6, A, C, K; folate; magnesium; phosphorus; copper; potassium; and manganese.

Mushrooms

Peppers

Roasted Corn with Poblano-Cilantro Butter (UNDER 30)

Sweet corn on the cob is rubbed with olive oil, salt, and pepper and then roasted in a hot oven until charred. When it's done, it's rolled in spicy, savory butter.

YIELD 6 EARS   SERVING 1 EAR   PREP 5 MINS   COOK 10 MINS

1 Preheat the oven to 425°F (220°C).

2 Place poblano pepper directly over the flame on a gas stove, or roast under the broiler as it preheats before you cook corn, turning to char on all sides. Transfer to a small bowl, cover with plastic wrap, and set aside to steam charred skin. After 5 minutes, remove plastic wrap. Core, seed, and peel poblano, and chop very finely (or pulse in the small bowl of a food processor until it's nearly smooth). Set aside.

3 Brush corn with extra-virgin olive oil, and sprinkle with kosher salt and black pepper. Place corn on a large rimmed baking sheet, and roast, turning once, for about 10 minutes or until tender and charred.

4 In a small bowl, stir chopped poblano into butter, and stir in cilantro and nutritional yeast.

5 Spread hot corn with poblano butter, and serve.

INGREDIENTS

1 poblano pepper

6 ears fresh corn, shucked and trimmed

1 TB. extra-virgin olive oil

½ tsp. kosher salt

½ tsp. freshly ground black pepper

¼ cup plant-based butter, softened

2 TB. finely chopped fresh cilantro

1 TB. nutritional yeast

If fresh corn on the cob is out of season, look for frozen bags of roasted corn at your supermarket. Heat and toss with poblano butter as directed. Leftover butter is fantastic with baked potatoes or steamed vegetables.

Sautéed Mushroom Medley

Sautéed mushrooms are so versatile—have them as a side dish, toss them with pasta, spread them on toasted French bread for crostini ... the possibilities are endless. Dried porcini mushrooms lend an earthy flavor to this dish, but if you don't have them, add an extra 4-ounce (110g) package of shiitakes.

YIELD 3 CUPS   SERVING ½ CUP   PREP 15 MINS   COOK 15 MINS

1   In a small bowl, place porcini mushrooms. Pour boiling water over top, and set aside to soak for about 5 minutes or until softened. Lift porcini from soaking water, agitating gently to release any soil. Chop mushrooms, and set aside. Reserve soaking water.

2   In a large sauté pan over medium-high heat, heat extra-virgin olive oil. Add shallots and garlic, and cook, stirring continuously, for 2 minutes. Adjust heat as necessary to prevent burning.

3   Add porcini, cremini mushrooms, white button mushrooms, shiitake mushrooms, rosemary, and thyme, and cook, stirring occasionally, for 10 minutes or until mushrooms begin to brown.

4   Season with kosher salt and black pepper, increase heat to high, and cook, stirring frequently, for 3 to 5 minutes or until mushrooms are golden brown and small bits are sticking to the pan.

5   Strain mushroom soaking liquid, leaving the last couple of teaspoons behind to eliminate grit. Add mushroom liquid and white wine all at once to deglaze the sauté pan, stirring vigorously to scrape up any browned bits on the bottom of the pan, and cook until all liquid is absorbed.

6   Remove from heat, stir in Italian flat-leaf parsley, and taste. Season with additional salt and pepper if desired, and serve immediately.

INGREDIENTS

.5 oz. (14g) dried porcini mushrooms

½ cup boiling water

3 TB. extra-virgin olive oil

2 shallots, finely chopped (¼ cup)

3 cloves garlic, minced

1 (8-oz.; 225g) pkg. cremini (baby bella) mushrooms, thinly sliced

1 (8-oz.; 225g) pkg. white button mushrooms, thinly sliced

1 (4-oz.; 110g) pkg. shiitake mushrooms, stemmed and thinly sliced

1 tsp. chopped fresh rosemary or ½ tsp. dried

1 tsp. chopped fresh thyme or ½ tsp. dried

1 tsp. kosher salt, or to taste

½ tsp. freshly ground black pepper, or to taste

2 TB. dry white wine

¼ cup finely chopped fresh Italian flat-leaf parsley

For *Mushroom Puffs*, roll out 1 sheet puff pastry on a flour-dusted surface. Spread cooled mushroom mixture evenly over pastry, sprinkle with ½ cup Cashew Ricotta, and roll from long end of pastry to form cylinder. Wrap in parchment paper and freeze until almost solid. To cook, remove parchment paper and cut into ¼-inch (.5cm) slices. Bake cut side down on a parchment paper-lined baking sheet at 400°F (200°C) for 10 minutes or until golden and puffed. Serve immediately.

Sesame Ginger Broccoli

Broccoli is quickly blanched to preserve its green color and crunch and then flavored with garlic and ginger for a simple, perfectly spiced plate of veggies.

1   Wash broccoli, and separate florets into small pieces. Peel broccoli stem, and slice into ¼-inch (.5cm) rounds.

2   Prepare an ice water bath for broccoli.

3   Bring a medium pot of water to a boil over high heat, and add kosher salt. Blanch broccoli and stems for 2 minutes or just until crisp-tender. Using tongs, immediately remove from boiling water and plunge into ice bath. Drain and set aside.

4   In a large sauté pan over medium-high heat, heat sesame oil. Add garlic and ginger, and stir for 1 minute.

5   Add broccoli, and cook for 2 minutes.

6   Sprinkle with gomasio, and serve immediately.

INGREDIENTS

1 large head fresh broccoli

1 tsp. kosher salt

2 TB. light sesame oil

2 cloves garlic, thinly sliced

1 tsp. freshly grated ginger

1 tsp. *gomasio*

Broccoli

Gomasio is a savory Japanese condiment made from roasted, unhulled sesame seeds and salt. Some varieties also contain seaweed. It's considered a healthier alternative to salt and brings a pleasant, nutty flavor to a dish. Try passing it at the table with noodle dishes, salads, or stir-fries.

Braised Brussels Sprouts with Chestnuts

This dish of golden brussels sprouts with the sweet, warm flavor of roasted chestnuts is best served in winter, when sprouts and chestnuts are in season. If you can't find fresh chestnuts, you can use jarred roasted, peeled chestnuts instead.

YIELD 4 CUPS **SERVING** ½ CUP **PREP** 5 MINS **COOK** 15 MINS

1 Preheat the oven to 400°F (200°C). Line a baking sheet with parchment paper.

2 In a large bowl, toss brussels sprouts with extra-virgin olive oil, balsamic vinegar, ½ teaspoon kosher salt, and black pepper. Spread sprouts on the prepared baking sheet, cut side down, and roast for 10 minutes.

3 In a large sauté pan over medium-high heat, heat butter. Stir in sugar, remaining ½ teaspoon kosher salt, and chestnuts. Cook, stirring, for 2 minutes.

4 Add brussels sprouts, and cook, stirring twice, for 2 minutes. Serve immediately.

INGREDIENTS

1 lb. (450g) fresh brussels sprouts, trimmed and halved

1 TB. extra-virgin olive oil

1 TB. balsamic vinegar

1 tsp. kosher salt

½ tsp. freshly ground black pepper

2 TB. plant-based butter

1 TB. sugar

1 cup roasted, peeled chestnuts, roughly chopped (about 18 chestnuts)

Look for firm chestnuts with a dark, glossy shell. To roast chestnuts, preheat the oven to 400°F (200°C). Score each chestnut with an X and spread on a baking sheet. Roast for about 10 minutes or until chestnuts split open. Let chestnuts cool until you can comfortably pick them up, and peel them. Eat out of hand or use in recipes. Store roasted chestnuts in the refrigerator in a tightly sealed glass jar for up to 2 weeks.

Stuffed Mushrooms

Aromatic vegetables, herbs, and mushroom stems are sautéed in plenty of olive oil; mixed with crunchy panko breadcrumbs; and baked in mushroom caps. Simple and simply delicious! Choose small mushrooms for this savory dish. They make little bites perfect for passing at parties.

YiELD 24 MUSHROOMS   **SERViNG** 4 MUSHROOMS   **PREP** 10 MiNS   **COOK** 35 MiNS

1   Preheat the oven to 400°F (200°C). Brush a baking dish just large enough to hold mushroom caps with 1 tablespoon extra-virgin olive oil.

2   Gently remove stems from white button mushroom caps. Place mushrooms in the prepared baking dish. Chop mushroom stems finely.

3   In a medium sauté pan over medium-high heat, heat 2 tablespoons extra-virgin olive oil. Add mushroom stems, red bell pepper, shallots, and garlic, and cook for about 5 minutes or until mushrooms begin to brown.

4   Deglaze the pan with 1 tablespoon white wine. Add panko breadcrumbs, Italian flat-leaf parsley, thyme, oregano, kosher salt, and black pepper, and remove from heat.

5   Pour remaining 3 tablespoons white wine in the baking dish around mushrooms. Evenly distribute filling among mushroom caps, lightly spooning a little filling into each. Drizzle remaining 2 tablespoons extra-virgin olive oil over mushroom caps.

6   Bake for 20 minutes or until mushrooms are tender and filling is golden. Serve hot, warm, or at room temperature.

INGREDiENTS

5 TB. extra-virgin olive oil

2 (10-oz.; 285g) pkg. white button mushrooms

¼ small red bell pepper, ribs and seeds removed, and finely chopped

2 small shallots, finely chopped

3 cloves garlic, finely chopped

4 TB. dry white wine

½ **cup** panko breadcrumbs

2 TB. finely chopped fresh Italian flat-leaf parsley

1 tsp. dried thyme

½ **tsp.** dried oregano

1 tsp. kosher salt

½ **tsp.** freshly ground black pepper

For a *"Cheesy" Stuffed Mushrooms* entrée, substitute 12 "stuffing-size" portobello mushrooms, and spoon 1 tablespoon Cashew Ricotta into the bottom of each mushroom cap before stuffing. Serve 3 or 4 mushrooms per person.

Minted Peas and Baby Potatoes

Sweet peas and tender new potatoes are tossed in a simple dressing of olive oil and fresh mint. Look for the tiniest potatoes you can find for this recipe.

YIELD 8 CUPS **SERVING** 1½ CUPS **PREP** 10 MINS **COOK** 10 MINS

1 In a large pot with a tight-fitting lid, bring 1 inch (2.5cm) water to a boil over medium heat. Place new potatoes in a steamer basket, set in the pot, and steam for about 10 minutes or until potatoes are tender and easily pierced with a fork. Drain and cool slightly. If potatoes are larger than 1 inch (2.5cm) in diameter, cut them in half.

2 Meanwhile, in a large saucepan over medium-high heat, heat extra-virgin olive oil. Add shallots and kosher salt, and cook for about 5 minutes or until softened.

3 Stir in peas and water, and cook for 2 minutes.

4 Add reserved potatoes, increase heat to high, and stir for 1 minute.

5 Remove from heat. Add mint, lemon juice, and black pepper, and serve.

INGREDIENTS

1 lb. (450g) very small new potatoes

2 TB. extra-virgin olive oil

1 shallot, thinly sliced (¼ cup)

1 tsp. kosher salt

4 cups shelled fresh peas, or 1 (10-oz.; 285g) pkg. frozen peas, thawed

2 TB. water

2 TB. finely chopped fresh mint

Juice of ½ lemon (1 TB.)

½ tsp. freshly ground black pepper

Peas

For *Herbed Peas and Potatoes,* replace mint with chervil, parsley, chives, French tarragon, or any combination of these herbs.

Sesame Asparagus

This recipe contains just a few ingredients but boasts huge flavor. Whether you grill or roast it, you'll love the counterpoint of sweet, tender asparagus with the warm flavors of sesame.

YIELD 1 POUND (450G) **SERVING** ¼ RECIPE **PREP** 5 MINS **COOK** 35 TO 40 MINS

1   Preheat the oven to 400°F (200°C), or preheat a grill for direct, high heat. Line a baking sheet with parchment paper.

2   Grasp an asparagus spear, and gently bend to snap off tough bottom of spear. Trim remaining spears to this length, and peel lower ²/₃ of asparagus stem. Place on the baking sheet, and toss with sesame oil, kosher salt, and black pepper.

3   Roast for 8 minutes, or grill over direct heat, turning once or twice, for about 5 minutes or until asparagus is tender. (When you pick up a single spear with a pair of tongs and it droops slightly, it's done.) Serve hot, warm, or cold, sprinkled with toasted sesame seeds.

INGREDIENTS

1 lb. (450g) slender asparagus spears

1 TB. dark sesame oil

1 tsp. kosher salt

½ tsp. freshly ground black pepper

1 TB. toasted sesame seeds or *gomasio*

For *Asian Asparagus,* add 1 teaspoon finely grated ginger and a drizzle of tamari. For *Lemon Garlic Asparagus,* replace sesame oil with extra-virgin olive oil, add 1 clove finely chopped garlic, and garnish with grated lemon zest instead of sesame seeds.

Latkes

Latkes are tender, crisp, freshly fried potato pancakes. They freeze fantastically, so you can make a big batch and heat them up whenever you want.

YiELD 20 LATKES   **SERViNG** 4 OR 5 LATKES   **PREP** 15 MiNS   **COOK** 10 MiNS

1   Place grated potatoes in a large, fine-mesh strainer, and use a handful of paper towels to press down on them, removing as much liquid as possible.

2   In a large bowl, whisk yellow onion, egg replacer, warm water, all-purpose flour, potato starch, kosher salt, and black pepper until completely smooth.

3   When potatoes are dry, quickly stir them together with onion mixture.

4   In a large, heavy frying pan over medium-high heat, heat ¼ cup grapeseed oil. Scoop ¼ cup measures of potato mixture into the pan, and press gently flat with a spatula. Fry for about 2 or 3 minutes or until golden brown, flip over, and fry the other side until golden. Remove to a metal cooling rack on a baking sheet and keep warm in the oven while you fry remaining batches, adding additional oil and adjusting heat as necessary.

5   Serve hot, with applesauce or plant-based sour cream.

INGREDiENTS

3 lb. (1.5kg) russet potatoes, peeled and grated

1 medium yellow onion, very finely chopped (in food processor if possible)

2 TB. egg replacer, such as Ener-G

3 TB. warm water

2 TB. all-purpose flour

2 TB. potato starch, or cornstarch

1 tsp. kosher salt

½ tsp. freshly ground black pepper

½ cup grapeseed oil

Applesauce or plant-based sour cream

Roasted Root Vegetable Medley

For this satisfying pan of root vegetables accented with fresh herbs and plenty of olive oil, choose a mix of carrots, celery root, potatoes, rutabaga, turnips, and parsnips.

YiELD 6 CUPS   **SERViNG** 1 CUP   **PREP** 20 MiNS   **COOK** 35 TO 40 MiNS

1   Preheat the oven to 400°F (200°C).

2   Place root vegetables in a 9×13-inch (23×33cm) glass baking pan, and drizzle extra-virgin olive oil evenly over top. Season with rosemary, thyme, sage, kosher salt, and black pepper, and toss with your hands to mix well.

3   Bake, uncovered and stirring once or twice, for 35 to 40 minutes or until vegetables are tender and turning dark golden brown at the edges. Serve hot or warm.

INGREDiENTS

6 cups assorted root vegetables, peeled and cut into 1-in. (2.5cm) chunks

½ cup extra-virgin olive oil

1 tsp. finely chopped fresh rosemary

1 tsp. fresh thyme leaves

1 tsp. fresh sage, finely chopped

1 tsp. kosher salt

½ tsp. freshly ground black pepper

SWEET POTATOES

Sweet potatoes are known for their orange flesh, but they also come in white, yellow, purple, and pink varieties. **Benefits** High in vitamin C, beta-carotene, and antioxidants; regulate blood sugar; improve skin health; and boost immunity. **Uses** Peak season is late summer and autumn; choose firm, fat, unblemished tubers that feel heavy for their size, and eat baked with plant-based butter and cinnamon, mashed, roasted in salads and casseroles, or simmered in soups and stews. **Recipes** Southern Sweet Potatoes with Pecan Streusel, Winter Vegetable Pot Pie.

Southern Sweet Potatoes with Pecan Streusel (T)

Creamy sweet potatoes are spiced with a touch of cinnamon and adorned with a sweet and savory pecan streusel topping in this classic casserole. You can easily double this recipe for a potluck or family meal.

YiELD 1 (8-iNCH; 20CM) CASSEROLE   **SERVING** ⅛ CASSEROLE   **PREP** 10 MiNS   **COOK** 50 MiNS

1. Preheat the oven to 350°F (180°C). Line a baking sheet with parchment paper. Lightly coat an 8×8-inch (20×20cm) baking pan with cooking spray.

2. In a large pot fitted with a steamer basket over medium-high heat, bring 1 inch (2.5cm) water to a boil. Place sweet potatoes in the basket, cover, and cook for 10 minutes or until potatoes are tender. Cool slightly.

3. Place sweet potatoes in a medium bowl, and using a potato masher, mash until smooth. Stir in 2 tablespoons butter, 2 tablespoons brown sugar, cinnamon, kosher salt, and black pepper. Spread sweet potato mixture evenly in the bottom of the baking pan.

4. To make streusel, in a medium bowl, combine all-purpose flour, remaining ¼ cup brown sugar, walnuts, and cayenne.

5. Cut remaining ¼ cup butter into small chunks, sprinkle over flour mixture, and use your hands to rub mixture until it begins to stick together. Sprinkle streusel over sweet potatoes, and bake for about 20 minutes or until golden. Serve immediately.

INGREDIENTS

2 lb. (450g) sweet potatoes, peeled and cut into 2-in. (5cm) chunks

2 TB. plus ¼ cup plant-based butter

2 TB. plus ¼ cup brown sugar, lightly packed

½ tsp. ground cinnamon

½ tsp. kosher salt

¼ tsp. freshly ground black pepper

¼ cup all-purpose flour

¼ cup chopped walnuts

Pinch cayenne

Mashing potatoes with a potato masher yields the best results. Try to avoid using your food processor or mixer because they can leave you with gummy potatoes. If you don't have a potato masher, use a large fork or pastry blender.

Casseroles and One-Pot Meals

You still can enjoy comfort food while eating a plant-based diet. Satisfy your craving for familiar flavors with a warm, hearty casserole, lasagna, or one-pot supper.

Winter Vegetable Pot Pie (T)

Lots of herb-seasoned veggies in a creamy sauce make this vegetable pot pie a comfort food favorite.

YiELD 1 (9x13-iNCH; 23x33CM) CASSEROLE   SERViNG ⅙ CASSEROLE   PREP 15 MiNS   COOK 45 MiNS

1   Preheat the oven to 400°F (200°C).

2   In a small saucepan over medium heat, heat 2 tablespoons grapeseed oil. Whisk in all-purpose flour until smooth, and cook, stirring constantly, for about 2 minutes or until flour is lightly golden and smells toasty.

3   Whisk in 2 cups Golden Chicken-y Stock, and simmer for 5 minutes. Remove from heat, and set aside.

4   In a wide sauté pan over medium-high heat, heat remaining 2 tablespoons grapeseed oil. Add yellow onion, celery, carrots, cremini mushrooms, and garlic, and cook, stirring frequently, for about 10 minutes, adjusting heat as necessary, or until vegetables are softened and beginning to color.

5   Stir in remaining 1 cup Golden Chicken-y Stock, red-skin potatoes, sweet potatoes, lima beans, bay leaf, thyme, kosher salt, and black pepper. Cover and cook, stirring once or twice and adding a bit of water if mixture seems dry, for 10 minutes.

6   Remove bay leaf, stir in reserved sauce, and pour vegetable mixture into a 9×13-inch (23×33cm) baking dish.

7   Roll out puff pastry on a floured surface to fit the top of the baking dish with an overhang of ½ inch (1.25cm). Dock pastry by pricking it all over with a fork, transfer it to the top of the baking dish, and lay it gently over vegetables. Tuck overhanging edge down into the inside of the baking dish.

8   Bake for about 30 minutes or until pastry is puffed and filling is hot and bubbly. Serve immediately.

INGREDIENTS

4 TB. grapeseed oil

3 TB. all-purpose flour

3 cups *Golden Chicken-y Stock*

1 large yellow onion, cut in small dice (1½ cups)

4 large stalks celery, cut in small dice (about 2 cups)

3 medium carrots, cut in small dice (2 cups)

1 (10-oz.; 285g) pkg. cremini (baby bella) mushrooms, quartered

3 cloves garlic, minced

4 large red-skin potatoes, cut in small dice (about 2 cups)

1 medium sweet potato, cut in small dice (about 1 cup)

2 cups frozen lima beans

1 bay leaf

1 tsp. dried thyme

1 tsp. kosher salt, plus more to taste

½ tsp. freshly ground black pepper

1 sheet puff pastry, thawed

For *Chicken-Style Pot Pie,* add 1 or 2 cups shredded Seitan. You also could add leafy greens such as lacinato kale to vegetables when you sauté them or make a package of your favorite stuffing mix to replace puff pastry topping and bake as directed.

Bisteeya (Moroccan Phyllo Pie)

Bisteeya, also known as *pastille,* is a dish of Berber origins often served at the beginning of a celebratory Moroccan meal. Layers of crisp phyllo and lightly sweetened almonds enclose a savory spiced filling of chickpeas and vegetables.

YIELD 1 (9-INCH; 23CM) PIE   **SERVING** ⅙ PIE   **PREP** 55 MINS   **COOK** 45 MINS

1 Preheat the oven to 400°F (200°C). Line a baking sheet with parchment paper.

2 In a wide sauté pan over medium-high heat, heat 2 tablespoons extra-virgin olive oil. Add red onions, garlic, ginger, and hot green chile, and cook, stirring frequently, for 10 minutes.

3 Add ½ teaspoon cinnamon, saffron threads, and Golden Chicken-y Stock, and bring to a boil. Stir in chickpeas, russet potato, and preserved lemon peel. Reduce heat to medium, and cook, stirring often, for about 10 minutes or until vegetables are very tender and most of liquid has evaporated.

4 Stir in cilantro, kosher salt, and black pepper, and set aside to cool.

5 Spread almonds on the prepared baking sheet, and toast in the oven for 6 minutes. Remove from the oven, and cool.

6 In a food processor fitted with a chopping blade, pulse together almonds, remaining ½ teaspoon cinnamon, and confectioners' sugar until mixture resembles fine crumbs.

7 Brush a 9-inch (23cm) round cake pan with a little extra-virgin olive oil. Lay 1 phyllo sheet in the pan, and sprinkle with ⅕ almond mixture. Brush a second sheet of phyllo with extra-virgin olive oil, and lay it oiled side up on top of second sheet in a criss-cross direction. Sprinkle with ¼ remaining almond mixture, and continue to layer remaining phyllo and almonds, placing phyllo so overhang is evenly spaced around the pan (first in a cross shape, then in an X shape, then a slightly offset X shape). Spoon vegetable-chickpea mixture into the pan and spread evenly. Gather overhanging phyllo to cover top of pie, and brush with a little more extra-virgin olive oil.

8 Place the pan on a rimmed baking sheet, and bake for about 35 minutes or until crisp and golden. Cool slightly, remove carefully from the pan, and dust with a little more confectioners' sugar and cinnamon. Cut into wedges, and serve.

INGREDIENTS

6 TB. extra-virgin olive oil

2 large red onions, finely chopped (3 cups)

2 cloves garlic, finely chopped

1 TB. grated fresh ginger

1 small hot green chile, seeded and finely chopped

1 tsp. ground cinnamon, plus more for dusting

½ tsp. saffron threads, crushed

1 cup *Golden Chicken-y Stock*

2 (14-oz.; 400g) cans chickpeas, rinsed and drained

1 russet potato, peeled and finely chopped (1½ cups)

1 preserved lemon, peel only, finely chopped

2 TB. finely chopped fresh cilantro

½ tsp. kosher salt

½ tsp. freshly ground black pepper

1 cup blanched almonds

1 TB. confectioners' sugar, plus more for dusting

6 (9×14-in.; 23×35.5cm) sheets phyllo dough

Savory Stuffed Cabbage

Cabbage rolls are incredibly flavorful Eastern European comfort food. Serve them with mashed potatoes and rye bread for a real treat.

YIELD 12 ROLLS   **SERVING** 2 OR 3 ROLLS   **PREP** 15 MINS PLUS 1 HOUR FREEZE TIME   **COOK** 40 MINS

1   Preheat the oven to 400°F (200°C). Lightly coat a 9×13-inch (23×33cm) glass baking pan with cooking spray.

2   Thaw napa cabbage leaves at room temperature, and squeeze excess moisture from each leaf. Set aside on a paper towel–lined surface.

3   In a large sauté pan over medium-high heat, heat extra-virgin olive oil. Add yellow onion, kosher salt, and black pepper, and stir for 2 minutes.

4   Add cremini mushrooms, and cook, stirring often, until they begin to color. Remove from heat, and stir in dill, Italian flat-leaf parsley, thyme, and brown rice.

5   In a small saucepan over medium-high heat, combine vegetable stock, tomato paste, sugar, allspice, and white wine. Bring to a boil, reduce heat to medium, and cook, stirring to dissolve tomato paste and white wine, for about 10 minutes or until sauce is reduced and slightly thickened. Keep warm while you fill cabbage rolls.

6   Working with 1 cabbage leaf at a time, spoon a few tablespoons filling in center and roll up like a burrito, tucking up short ends first, then rolling each into a long cylinder. Place each finished cabbage roll in the prepared baking dish, and repeat with remaining ingredients.

7   Pour sauce over cabbage rolls, cover the pan with heavy-duty aluminum foil, and bake for 30 minutes. Serve hot.

INGREDIENTS

12 large napa cabbage leaves, bottom 3 in. (7.5cm) of stem removed, frozen for at least 1 hour

2 TB. extra-virgin olive oil

1 small yellow onion, finely chopped (¾ cup)

1 tsp. kosher salt

¼ tsp. freshly ground black pepper

1 (8-oz.; 225g) pkg. cremini (baby bella) mushrooms, finely chopped

1 TB. finely chopped fresh dill

1 TB. finely chopped fresh Italian flat-leaf parsley

½ tsp. dried thyme leaves

1 cup cooked brown rice

2 cups vegetable stock

4 TB. tomato paste

2 TB. sugar

½ tsp. ground allspice

¼ cup dry white wine

Cabbage leaves

Vegetable Enchiladas with Roasted Tomato Sauce Ⓣ

A filling of tender vegetables is wrapped in tortillas and baked in a savory sauce of roasted tomatoes. This dish has a mild chile flavor and freezes beautifully.

YIELD 16 ENCHILADAS   **SERVING** 3 ENCHILADAS   **PREP** 45 MINS   **COOK** 1 HOUR, 40 MINS

1 Preheat the oven to 375°F (190°C). Lightly coat a 9×13-inch (23×33cm) baking pan with a little extra-virgin olive oil.

2 Cut tomatoes in half, place in the baking pan, and toss with 2 tablespoons extra-virgin olive oil, red bell pepper strips, ½ teaspoon kosher salt, and oregano. Roast for 1 hour, stirring occasionally, and cool slightly.

3 Purée tomato mixture, vegetable stock, and New Mexico chile powder in batches in a blender or a food processor. Set aside.

4 In a wide sauté pan over medium-high heat, heat remaining 2 tablespoons extra-virgin olive oil. Add yellow onion and poblano chile peppers, and cook, stirring occasionally, for 4 or 5 minutes, adjusting heat as necessary.

5 Add garlic, and stir for 1 minute. Add zucchini, and cook for about 4 or 5 minutes or until vegetables are golden. Stir in roasted corn, and cook another 1 or 2 minutes. Stir in black beans, cilantro, remaining ½ teaspoon kosher salt, and ½ cup reserved sauce, and remove from heat.

6 Spread ½ cup sauce on the bottom of the prepared baking pan. Spoon about 1/12 of filling into center of 1 tortilla, filling it generously, gently roll, and place in the pan. Repeat with remaining tortillas and filling, fitting them very snugly into the pan. Pour some of remaining sauce over top of enchiladas, lightly covering them while leaving edges exposed, and sprinkle with pepper jack–style cheese (if using). Cover with aluminum foil, and bake for about 40 minutes or until hot and bubbly. Serve immediately.

For *Tortilla Soup,* stir 2 cups sauce into 2 cups vegetable stock. Heat and stir in 1 cup lightly crushed tortilla chips and 1 cup black beans. Serve topped with a spoonful of plant-based sour cream and diced avocado.

INGREDIENTS

2 (10-oz.; 285g) pkg. cocktail-size tomatoes, such as Campari

4 TB. extra-virgin olive oil

2 medium red bell peppers, ribs and seeds removed, and cut in 1-in. (2.5cm) strips

1 tsp. kosher salt

½ tsp. dried oregano

2 cups vegetable stock

3 TB. dried New Mexico chile powder

1 large yellow onion, finely chopped (1½ cups)

2 poblano chile peppers, seeded and finely chopped

2 cloves garlic, finely chopped

2 large zucchini, cut in ½-in. (1.25cm) dice

1 (1 lb.; 450g) pkg. roasted corn kernels, or regular frozen corn kernels

1 (14-oz.; 400g) can black beans, rinsed and drained

2 TB. finely chopped fresh cilantro

16 (6-in.; 15.25cm) handmade-style corn and wheat blend tortillas

½ cup shredded plant-based pepper jack–style cheese (optional)

Mushroom Lasagna

The meaty flavor of mushrooms blends perfectly with Cashew Ricotta and zesty Tomato Sauce. No-boil lasagna noodles make this an easy weeknight dish.

YIELD 1 (9×13-INCH; 23×33CM) LASAGNA   **SERVING** ⅛ LASAGNA   **PREP** 30 MINS   **COOK** 50 MINS

1 Preheat the oven to 375°F (190°C). Lightly coat a 9×13-inch (23×33cm) baking dish with cooking spray.

2 Place porcini mushrooms in a small bowl, pour boiling water over top, and soak for about 5 minutes or until softened. Lift porcini from soaking water, agitating gently to release any soil. Reserve soaking liquid. Chop mushrooms, and set aside.

3 In a large sauté pan over medium-high heat, heat extra-virgin olive oil. Add garlic, and cook, stirring continuously, for 1 minute.

4 Add porcini mushrooms, cremini mushrooms, shiitake mushrooms, rosemary, kosher salt, oregano, and black pepper, and cook, stirring occasionally, for 10 minutes or until mushrooms begin to brown.

5 Strain mushroom soaking liquid, leaving the last few teaspoons behind to eliminate grit, and add to mushrooms along with red wine, stirring vigorously to deglaze the pan. Stir until liquid has evaporated, and set mushrooms aside.

6 Spread 1 cup Tomato Sauce evenly over the bottom of the baking dish, lay 3 lasagna noodles over sauce, spoon ½ of mushroom mixture and ½ of Cashew Ricotta evenly over noodles. Pour ¾ cup Tomato Sauce over Cashew Ricotta, layer 3 more noodles, add remaining mushrooms and Cashew Ricotta, followed by another cup of Tomato Sauce. Finish with another 3 noodles and 1 cup Tomato Sauce. Cover the pan with heavy-duty aluminum foil, folding back 1 corner slightly to vent. Reserve remaining ½ cup sauce for serving.

7 Bake for 50 minutes or until hot and bubbly. Remove from the oven and set aside to rest for 5 minutes before cutting. Reheat remaining sauce to pass at table.

INGREDIENTS

½ oz. (14g) dried porcini mushrooms

½ cup boiling water

¼ cup extra-virgin olive oil

3 cloves garlic, minced

1 (8-oz.; 225g) pkg. cremini (baby bella) mushrooms, thinly sliced

1 (4-oz.; 110g) pkg. shiitake mushrooms, stemmed and thinly sliced

1 tsp. chopped fresh rosemary or ½ tsp. dried

1 tsp. kosher salt, or to taste

½ tsp. dried oregano

½ tsp. freshly ground black pepper, or to taste

¼ cup dry red wine

4 cups *Tomato Sauce*

9 no-boil lasagna noodles

2 cups *Cashew Ricotta*

Summer Squash and Onion Bake

Tender zucchini and yellow summer squash slices are bathed in a creamy béchamel sauce with plenty of sweet onions and then topped with breadcrumbs and baked until golden.

YIELD 1 (8-INCH; 20CM) CASSEROLE   SERVING ¼ TO ⅙ CASSEROLE   PREP 15 MINS   COOK 40 MINS

1   Preheat the oven to 350°F (180°C). Lightly grease an 8×8-inch (20×20cm) square baking dish.

2   In a wide sauté pan over medium-high heat, heat 2 tablespoons extra-virgin olive oil. Add sweet onions, and cook, stirring, for 5 minutes or until softened.

3   Add garlic, and stir for 1 minute. Remove onions and garlic from the pan, and keep warm.

4   Add 1 tablespoon olive oil, zucchini, and yellow squash, and season with kosher salt and black pepper. Increase heat to high, and cook, stirring every minute or so, for 5 minutes or until vegetables begin to turn golden.

5   Sprinkle with all-purpose flour, reduce heat to medium, and stir for 1 minute to combine well. Return onion mixture to the pan.

6   Stir in nondairy milk, nutmeg, and rosemary. Bring to a boil, and cook for about 2 minutes or until thickened. Remove from heat.

7   In a small bowl, combine panko breadcrumbs, chives, thyme, and remaining 1 tablespoon extra-virgin olive oil.

8   Pour squash mixture into the baking dish, spread gently, and sprinkle evenly with breadcrumb mixture. Bake, uncovered, for 30 minutes. Serve immediately.

INGREDIENTS

4 TB. extra-virgin olive oil

2 large sweet onions, such as Vidalia, thinly sliced into rings

2 cloves garlic, finely chopped

2 medium zucchini, thinly sliced

2 medium yellow squash, thinly sliced

1 tsp. kosher salt

¼ tsp. freshly ground black pepper

2 TB. all-purpose flour

1½ cups nondairy milk, such as rice or soy

¼ tsp. ground nutmeg

½ tsp. finely chopped fresh rosemary

1 cup panko breadcrumbs

2 TB. finely chopped fresh chives

1 tsp. dried thyme

Rosemary

For a *"Cheesy" Vegetable Bake,* gently stir in 1 cup of your favorite shredded plant-based cheese into vegetables and sauce before baking.

Eggplant and Roasted Tomato Polenta Lasagna

It takes some time to assemble this dish, but the savory flavors of roasted eggplant, tomatoes, pesto, toasted pine nuts, and creamy polenta are worth it. You won't miss the cheese or saturated fat in this flavor-packed dish.

YIELD 1 (9-INCH; 23CM) LASAGNA   SERVING ⅙ LASAGNA   PREP 45 MINS PLUS COOL TIME   COOK 45 MINS

1 Line a 9×9-inch (23×23cm) baking pan with parchment paper, and brush it with a little olive oil.

2 In a large saucepan over high heat, bring water to a boil. Stirring constantly, add polenta in a thin stream. Add ½ teaspoon kosher salt, reduce heat to medium, and continue to stir until polenta is fully cooked. (It will be creamy and smooth with no "bite" when you taste it.)

3 Pour polenta into the prepared baking pan, and allow to cool for a bit. Cover and refrigerate for at least 2 hours or overnight or until set.

4 Preheat the oven to 400°F (200°C).

5 Sprinkle Italian eggplant chunks with ½ teaspoon kosher salt and place in a colander to drain for 30 minutes. Rinse, and gently squeeze out any remaining water.

6 On a large rimmed baking sheet, toss eggplant cubes and cherry tomatoes with sliced garlic and 3 tablespoons extra-virgin olive oil. Spread evenly, and roast, stirring once or twice, for 30 minutes. Remove from the oven, and reduce the temperature to 375°F (190°C).

7 When polenta has set, carefully turn it out of the pan. Cut into thirds, and slice each third horizontally into 3 equal pieces so you have 9 polenta "lasagna noodles." Handle carefully using a spatula, but don't worry if they break—just fit them back together in the pan.

8 To assemble lasagna, brush the baking pan with remaining 1 tablespoon extra-virgin olive oil. Spread ½ cup Tomato Sauce over bottom of pan, and cover bottom of pan with 3 pieces of polenta. Top with ½ of tomato-eggplant mixture and ½ of Summer Pesto, followed by another layer of polenta. Add another ½ cup Tomato Sauce, remaining eggplant-tomato mixture, and remaining Summer Pesto. Top with final layer of polenta, and spread remaining Tomato Sauce evenly over top. Cover and bake for about 40 minutes or until hot and bubbly.

9 Just before serving, sprinkle basil and toasted pine nuts over top of lasagna. Serve hot.

INGREDIENTS

5 cups water

1 cup coarse polenta (not instant)

1½ tsp. kosher salt

1 large Italian eggplant, cut in 1-in. (2.5cm) cubes

12 oz. (340g) cherry tomatoes, halved

3 cloves garlic, thinly sliced

4 TB. extra-virgin olive oil

1½ cups *Tomato Sauce*

1 cup *Summer Pesto*

6 large basil leaves, cut in thin ribbons (chiffonade)

½ cup pine nuts, toasted

Tamale Casserole

A tender crust of cornmeal and masa harina encloses a slightly spicy, savory filling of veggies and pinto beans in this lighter version of a tamale casserole.

YiELD 1 (9×13-INCH; 23×33CM) CASSEROLE SERViNG ⅙ CASSEROLE PREP 10 MiNS COOK 80 MiNS

1 Preheat the oven to 375°F (190°C). Lightly oil a 9×13-inch (23×33cm) baking dish.

2 In a large sauté pan over medium-high heat, heat 3 tablespoons extra-virgin olive oil. Add yellow onion, green bell pepper, and garlic, and cook for 3 minutes, adjusting heat as needed to prevent burning.

3 Add cumin, oregano, chipotle chile, adobo sauce, and lacinato kale, and cook, stirring frequently, for 5 minutes.

4 Stir in pinto beans, diced tomatoes with juice, vegetable stock, and pimiento-stuffed green olives, and cook for 10 minutes or until all vegetables are tender and sauce has reduced slightly.

5 Meanwhile, in a large saucepan over high heat, bring water to a boil. Stir in kosher salt, and slowly whisk in yellow cornmeal and masa harina. Reduce heat to medium, and cook, stirring frequently, for 15 minutes.

6 Stir in corn and remaining 1 tablespoon extra-virgin olive oil.

7 Spoon ½ of cornmeal mixture into the bottom of the prepared baking dish, and spread evenly. Top with vegetables, followed by remaining cornmeal mixture. Sprinkle cheddar-style cheese over top, and bake for 40 minutes. Serve immediately.

INGREDiENTS

4 TB. extra-virgin olive oil

1 large yellow onion, finely chopped (1½ cups)

1 medium green bell pepper, ribs and seeds removed, and finely chopped (1 cup)

3 cloves garlic, finely chopped

1 tsp. ground cumin

½ tsp. dried oregano

1 canned chipotle chile in adobo, finely chopped

2 TB. adobo sauce (from canned chile)

1 bunch lacinato kale, tough stems removed, and roughly chopped

2 (14-oz.; 400g) cans pinto beans, rinsed and drained

1 (14-oz.; 400g) can diced tomatoes, with juice

1 cup vegetable stock

¼ cup chopped pimiento-stuffed green olives

5½ cups water

2½ tsp. kosher salt

¾ cup coarse yellow cornmeal

½ cup masa harina

1½ cups fresh or frozen corn kernels

1 cup shredded plant-based cheddar-style cheese

Green bell pepper

Using a mixture of coarse cornmeal and masa harina gives this dish great tamale flavor, but you can use a total of 1¼ cups cornmeal if you don't have masa harina. If your grocery store carries roasted corn in the freezer section, it adds fantastic flavor to this dish. An unbaked casserole can be frozen for up to 3 months and baked from frozen at 350°F (180°C).

Mixed Vegetable Cottage Pie

This rich, intensely flavored comfort food favorite is sure to please. Substitute parsnips for rutabaga in the topping if you like.

YIELD 1 (2-QUART; 2L) CASSEROLE   SERVING ¼ CASSEROLE   PREP 30 MINS   COOK 1 HOUR

1   In a large saucepan over medium-high heat, heat vegetable oil. Add yellow onion, and sauté, stirring, for 3 minutes or until lightly golden.

2   Add white mushrooms, carrots, turnips, peas, and pinto beans. Stir in vegetable stock, soy sauce, vegan Worcestershire sauce, herbes de Provence, kosher salt, and black pepper. Bring to a boil, reduce heat to medium, cover, and simmer gently for 10 minutes or until vegetables are tender.

3   In a small bowl, blend all-purpose flour with water. Stir mixture into the saucepan, and cook, stirring constantly, for 2 minutes to thicken.

4   Meanwhile, cook rutabaga and potatoes in a large saucepan of salted, boiling water over medium-high heat for 15 minutes or until tender. Drain and return vegetables to the saucepan, reduce heat to low, and cook to dry out slightly.

5   Add plant-based butter, rice milk, a generous grating of nutmeg, and a generous grinding of black pepper, and mash. Beat well with a wooden spoon until smooth.

6   Preheat the oven to 375°F (190°C).

7   Spoon vegetable and bean mixture into a 2-quart (2L) ovenproof baking dish or 4 ramekins. Top with rutabaga mash, and fluff with a fork. Sprinkle cheddar-style cheese (if using) over top, and bake for about 40 minutes or until golden. Serve hot.

INGREDIENTS

1 TB. vegetable oil

1 medium yellow onion, finely chopped (1 cup)

4 oz. (110g) white mushrooms, sliced

2 medium carrots, grated (1 cup)

2 small turnips, grated (2 cups)

2 oz. (55g) shelled fresh or thawed frozen peas

2 (14-oz.; 400g) cans pinto beans, rinsed and drained

2 cups vegetable stock

1 TB. soy sauce

1 TB. vegan Worcestershire sauce, such as Annie's

1 tsp. herbes de Provence

½ tsp. kosher salt

¼ tsp. freshly ground black pepper, plus more to taste

¼ cup all-purpose flour

¼ cup water

1 small rutabaga, cut into small chunks (2 cups)

1 lb. (450g) russet potatoes, peeled and cut into small chunks

2 TB. plant-based butter

¼ cup rice milk

Grated nutmeg

2 oz. (55g) grated plant-based cheddar-style cheese (optional)

Not all Worcestershire sauce is plant-based, so read the ingredients. Look for an organic brand made without anchovies, such as Annie's.

Cassoulet

This slow-cooked comfort-food dish is perfect to pop in the oven on a snowy day. Fresh thyme, herbes de Provence, red wine, and aromatic vegetables slowly infuse creamy beans with flavor. Serve steaming bowls of this delicious stew with a simple salad and plenty of crusty French bread.

YIELD 6 CUPS   SERVING 1½ CUPS   PREP 15 MINS   COOK 3 HOURS, 45 MINS

1 Preheat the oven to 300°F (150°C).

2 Rinse white beans, pick over, and drain.

3 In a heavy earthenware or cast-iron Dutch oven with a lid, combine beans and vegetable stock. (Alternatively, you can use a heavy stainless-steel Dutch oven with a lid.) Set aside.

4 In a medium sauté pan over medium-high heat, heat extra-virgin olive oil. Add leeks, celery, carrot, and shallot, and stir for 5 minutes.

5 Stir in garlic, thyme, and herbes de Provence, and cook for 1 minute.

6 Stir in tomato paste, followed by red wine, kosher salt, and black pepper. Combine thoroughly, and remove from heat.

7 Pour vegetable mixture over beans, stir gently, and bake, covered, stirring once or twice, for 3½ hours or until beans are tender. Remove the lid during the last hour of cooking.

8 Remove from the oven, stir in Italian flat-leaf parsley, and serve.

INGREDIENTS

2 cups dried white beans, such as flageolet or great northern

4 cups vegetable stock, preferably homemade

½ cup extra-virgin olive oil

2 medium leeks, white and light green parts, cut into $^1/_8$-in. (3mm) pieces (2 cups)

3 medium stalks celery, cut into $^1/_8$-in. (3mm) pieces (1 cup)

1 medium carrot, halved and cut into $^1/_8$-in. (3mm) slices (1 cup)

2 medium shallots, minced (½ cup)

2 cloves garlic, thinly sliced

1 TB. fresh thyme leaves

1 tsp. herbes de Provence

2 TB. tomato paste

1½ cups dry red wine

1 tsp. kosher salt

½ tsp. freshly ground black pepper

½ cup finely chopped fresh Italian flat-leaf parsley

For *Slow Cooker Cassoulet*, combine beans and vegetable broth in a 4-quart (4L) slow cooker, and set heat to low. Sauté vegetables as directed, add to the slow cooker, cover, and cook for 8 hours or until beans are tender.

Butternut Squash Tagine

A *tagine* is a Moroccan specialty dish as well as the container it's cooked in. If you have a tagine, use it to cook and serve this fragrant, gently spiced, warming stew. If not, a skillet with a lid works just fine.

YIELD 6 CUPS   SERVING 1½ CUPS   PREP 20 MINS   COOK 25 MINS

1   In a tagine or a large skillet with a lid over medium-high heat, heat extra-virgin olive oil. Add butternut squash and yellow onion, and cook, stirring, for 5 minutes.

2   Add garlic, preserved lemon peel, tomato paste, cumin, coriander, cinnamon, and black pepper, and stir for 1 minute.

3   Stir in kosher salt, vegetable stock, chickpeas, and apricots. Cover, reduce heat to low or medium-low, and cook at a brisk simmer, stirring occasionally, for 15 to 20 minutes or until squash is tender but not mushy.

4   Add green olives, garnish with cilantro, and serve.

INGREDIENTS

2 TB. extra-virgin olive oil

1 medium butternut squash, peeled and cut into ½-in. (1.25cm) cubes

1 large yellow onion, halved and thinly sliced

2 cloves garlic, finely chopped

½ preserved lemon, peel only, finely chopped

1 TB. tomato paste

1 tsp. ground cumin

1 tsp. ground coriander

½ tsp. ground cinnamon

½ tsp. freshly ground black pepper

1 tsp. kosher salt

2 cups vegetable stock

1 (14-oz.; 400g) can chickpeas, rinsed and drained

½ cup dried apricots, chopped

½ cup pitted green olives

¼ cup finely chopped fresh cilantro

If you can't find preserved lemon at your grocery store or specialty shop, substitute by adding 1 tablespoon freshly squeezed lemon juice along with vegetable stock.

Seeds, Grains, and Pasta

When you want to feed a crowd, look no further. The pasta, risotto, paella, and quinoa dishes here are sure to please. Feeling adventurous? Make your own ravioli!

Crispy Quinoa Cakes

Quinoa and lentils form a crispy exterior and tender interior in these savory little bites. Feel free to mix up the spices—add curry and ginger for an Indian-inspired flavor, or replace the cilantro and cumin with basil and lemon zest for Italian flair.

YiELD 12 CAKES **SERViNG** 2 CAKES **PREP** 25 MiNS **COOK** 25 MiNS

1 Preheat the oven to 400°F (200°C). Line a baking sheet with parchment paper.

2 In a small bowl, whisk together flax meal and warm water. Set aside.

3 In a medium sauté pan over medium-high heat, heat 2 tablespoons extra-virgin olive oil. When oil begins to shimmer, add red onion and cook, stirring frequently, for about 3 minutes or until onion is translucent and just beginning to turn golden around edges.

4 Add garlic, reduce heat to medium, and stir for 30 seconds. Add lacinato kale, and cook, stirring occasionally, for about 5 minutes. Remove from heat, and set aside to cool slightly.

5 In a large bowl, combine quinoa, lentils, pumpkin seeds, Italian flat-leaf parsley, and cilantro.

6 Whisk tahini, lemon juice, and all-purpose flour into flax mixture until smooth, and add to quinoa mixture. Stir in kosher salt, cumin, black pepper, and kale mixture, and combine well.

7 Using wet hands, divide mixture into 12 even-size balls, and flatten into 1-inch (2.5cm) cakes, spacing them evenly on the baking sheet. (If desired, you can use a ring mold to form perfectly round cakes.)

8 Brush each cake lightly with remaining extra-virgin olive oil, and bake for 20 minutes or until golden brown and crisp. Serve immediately.

INGREDiENTS

2 TB. flax meal (ground flaxseeds)

6 TB. warm water

3 TB. extra-virgin olive oil

¼ medium red onion, finely chopped (¼ cup)

2 cloves garlic, finely chopped

1 bunch lacinato kale, stemmed and finely chopped

2 cups cooked quinoa

1½ cups cooked brown or green lentils

¼ cup roasted pumpkin seeds, roughly chopped

¼ cup finely chopped fresh Italian flat-leaf parsley

2 TB. finely chopped fresh cilantro

2 TB. tahini

Juice of 1 lemon (2 TB.)

2 TB. all-purpose flour

1 tsp. kosher salt

1 tsp. ground cumin

½ tsp. freshly ground black pepper

For *Gluten-Free Quinoa Cakes*, simply use gluten-free flour instead of all-purpose. Serve these protein-packed patties on salad, in a pita, add Guacamole or Romesco Sauce, or drizzle with lemon juice and tahini.

QUINOA

Quinoa's high protein and healthy fat content make it a nutritious and filling choice for main and side dishes. This ancient seed, often thought of as a grain, is also rich in calcium and iron. **Benefits** Gluten free, good source of protein, promotes heart health, contains antioxidants. **Uses** Quinoa has a springy texture and a grassy, slightly bitter flavor. Toast it in a dry pan, add water, and steam as you would rice. Available in whole-grain seeds, flour, or flakes, it goes well with apples, black beans, chiles, cilantro, corn, grapes, nuts, oranges, squash, and sweet potatoes. **Recipes** Crispy Quinoa Cakes, Quinoa Vegetable Salad.

Quinoa Vegetable Salad (T)

Nutty quinoa teams up with edamame, kale, and crunchy jicama for a protein-packed powerhouse of a salad that's perfect for lunches, picnics, and potluck suppers.

YIELD 8 CUPS   SERVING 2 CUPS   PREP 10 MINS   COOK 25 MINS

1   In a dry, medium saucepan with a tight-fitting lid over medium-high heat, toast quinoa, stirring constantly, for 1 minute.

2   Add water and ½ teaspoon kosher salt. Bring to a boil, reduce heat to low, and cook, covered, for 15 minutes. Let stand covered for 10 minutes, and fluff with a fork.

3   In a large bowl, toss curly kale leaves with 1 tablespoon lemon juice, 1 tablespoon extra-virgin olive oil, and a pinch of kosher salt. Using clean hands, massage kale for 5 minutes or until softened and reduced. Stir in garlic, and set aside.

4   In a small bowl, whisk remaining 1 tablespoon lemon juice, remaining 2 tablespoons extra-virgin olive oil, remaining ½ teaspoon kosher salt, apple cider vinegar, and tahini. Set aside.

5   Add quinoa, jicama, edamame, red onion, almonds, cranberries, and reserved dressing to kale, and toss. Serve warm or cold.

INGREDIENTS

1 cup quinoa

1½ cups water

1 tsp. kosher salt

1 bunch curly kale, leaves only

Juice of 1 lemon (2 TB.)

3 TB. extra-virgin olive oil

1 clove garlic, finely chopped

2 TB. apple cider vinegar

2 TB. tahini

1 small jicama, cut in ¼-in. (.5cm) dice (about 2 cups)

1 cup frozen, fully cooked edamame, thawed

½ small red onion, very thinly sliced

½ cup toasted sliced almonds

½ cup dried cranberries

For *Gluten-Free Quinoa Vegetable Salad,* replace edamame with 1 cup cooked lima beans.

Risotto Milanese

Golden, saffron-scented rice is slowly stirred with stock to gradually release the rice's starch, resulting in a comforting, creamy-tasting, plant-based version of a beloved Italian classic.

YIELD 6 TO 8 CUPS **SERVING** 1½ CUPS **PREP** 5 MINS **COOK** 35 MINS

1 In a large, wide saucepan over medium heat, heat extra-virgin olive oil. Add shallots and kosher salt, and cook, stirring frequently, for about 10 minutes or until shallots are softened and just beginning to turn a light golden color (without browning).

2 In a large saucepan over medium-high heat, heat Golden Chicken-y Stock. Reduce heat to a simmer.

3 In a small bowl, place saffron threads. Ladle about 1 tablespoon stock over saffron, and set aside to steep.

4 Increase heat under shallots to high, add Arborio rice all at once, and cook, stirring constantly, for 2 minutes or until rice smells nutty.

5 Add white wine and saffron, reduce heat to medium, and stir until most of wine has been absorbed.

6 Add 2 cups simmering stock to the pan, and reduce heat to low or medium-low. (Adjust heat as needed to keep risotto at a gentle simmer as you cook it.) Cook, stirring constantly until stock is almost completely absorbed, and add another cup of stock. Continue in this manner until rice is tender but *al dente* (still a bit firm to the bite) and risotto is creamy.

7 Remove from heat, stir in nutritional yeast, butter, Italian flat-leaf parsley, chives, and black pepper. Taste and add more kosher salt if desired, and serve immediately.

INGREDIENTS

3 TB. extra-virgin olive oil

4 small shallots, finely minced (½ cup)

1 tsp. kosher salt, plus more to taste

8 cups *Golden Chicken-y Stock* or homemade vegetable stock

¼ tsp. saffron threads

2 cups Arborio or carnaroli rice

1 cup dry white wine

2 TB. nutritional yeast

1 TB. plant-based butter

1 TB. finely chopped fresh Italian flat-leaf parsley

1 TB. finely chopped fresh chives

½ tsp. freshly ground black pepper

For *"Cheesy" Risotto*, stir in ½ cup Cashew Ricotta just before serving. For *Lemon Asparagus Risotto*, stir in peas or thinly sliced asparagus with 1 teaspoon lemon zest. For *Mushroom Risotto*, replace stock with Mushroom Stock, and stir in some Sautéed Mushroom Medley.

Moroccan Couscous

Try this fluffy grain as a side dish with tempeh or tofu, or top it with a vegetable stew such as Butternut Squash Tagine.

YIELD 4 CUPS   **SERVING** 1 CUP   **PREP** 10 MINS   **COOK** 30 MINS

1 In a medium saucepan over medium heat, heat extra-virgin olive oil. Add yellow onion, and cook, stirring occasionally, for 10 minutes.

2 Stir in cumin, turmeric, kosher salt, cinnamon stick, and saffron threads, and cook for 30 seconds.

3 Add Golden Chicken-y Stock, reduce heat to low, and simmer for 10 minutes.

4 In a small bowl, place apricots and currants. Add ¼ cup hot stock, cover, and set aside.

5 Measure remaining stock to be sure you have exactly 2 cups. Return stock to the saucepan, and bring to a boil over high heat. Remove from heat, stir in couscous, cover, and set aside for 10 minutes.

6 Drain apricots and currants. Remove cinnamon stick from couscous, and fluff couscous with a fork. Stir fruit and pine nuts into couscous, garnish with cilantro, and serve immediately.

INGREDIENTS

2 TB. extra-virgin olive oil

1 medium yellow onion, halved and thinly sliced

½ tsp. ground cumin

½ tsp. ground turmeric

½ tsp. kosher salt

1 (3- or 4-in.; 7.5 to 10cm) cinnamon stick

½ tsp. saffron threads, lightly crushed

2½ cups *Golden Chicken-y Stock* or vegetable stock

¼ cup chopped dried apricots

¼ cup currants

1 cup instant couscous

½ cup toasted pine nuts

1 TB. finely chopped fresh cilantro

Dried apricots

Traditional Moroccan couscous is steamed over a pan of flavorful liquid and cooled and rubbed by hand several times, resulting in a fluffy grain that grows to several times its original size. You can avoid this time-consuming process by purchasing unseasoned instant couscous (the kind in boxes at the supermarket), which has already been steamed and dried.

Arancini (Risotto Balls) Ⓣ

These crunchy-on-the-outside, creamy-on-the-inside rice balls are the perfect choice to serve at a party when you want to indulge yourself and your guests. Or enjoy risotto for supper one night, and have *arancini* on the side with a bowl of soup or a salad later in the week.

YiELD 12 BALLS   **SERViNG** 2 BALLS   **PREP** 45 MiNS   **COOK** 10 MiNS

1 Line two baking sheets with parchment paper.

2 Place all-purpose flour, water, and panko breadcrumbs in separate small, shallow bowls.

3 Scoop out ½ cup portions of chilled Risotto Milanese. Using wet hands, form each portion into a ball, tucking 1 mozzarella cheese cube and a few peas into center. Place balls on a baking sheet.

4 Working one at a time, quickly roll each ball in flour, dip in water, and roll in panko breadcrumbs, being sure to thoroughly coat each ball. Roll once more in flour, shake off excess, and set aside on the second baking sheet. When all balls are breaded, chill for 30 minutes or overnight.

5 Just before you're ready to serve, preheat the oven to 250°F (120°C).

6 In a wide saucepan over medium-high heat, heat 3 or 4 inches (7.5 to 10cm) grapeseed oil. Use a deep-frying thermometer to bring oil to 375°F (190°C), and add balls, 3 or 4 at a time. Cook, turning frequently, for about 3 minutes or until golden brown all over. Transfer to a metal cooling rack set over a baking pan to keep balls crisp, and keep warm in the oven as you fry subsequent batches. Serve hot with Tomato Sauce for dipping.

INGREDIENTS

1 cup all-purpose flour

½ cup water

1½ cups panko breadcrumbs

½ batch *Risotto Milanese*, or 5 cups your favorite risotto, chilled overnight

10 (½-in.; 1.25cm) cubes plant-based mozzarella cheese

¼ cup frozen peas

Grapeseed oil

Tomato Sauce

Declare one evening a week "leftover night" when all leftovers are eaten, or have fun creating something new out of your remnants from earlier meals. One of my favorite leftover meals was tacos made from beans and veggies I scooped out of soup. Stir leftovers into polenta, or mix with pasta and bake in a casserole. Leftover tofu, tempeh, or seitan make a great sandwich filling.

Farro Risotto with Roasted Fennel and Mushrooms

Farro is an ancient grain. It's a type of wheat that yields a firm bite and a nutty flavor—the perfect foil for sweet roasted fennel and meaty mushrooms.

YIELD 6 CUPS   SERVING 1½ CUPS   PREP 10 MINS   COOK 35 MINS

1 Preheat the oven to 400°F (200°C). Line a rimmed baking sheet with parchment paper.

2 In a medium saucepan over high heat, combine farro with 1 teaspoon kosher salt and enough water to cover by 1 inch (2.5cm). Bring to a boil, reduce heat to medium, and cook, stirring occasionally, for 20 minutes. (Adjust heat as necessary to maintain a brisk simmer.) Drain and set aside.

3 On the baking sheet, toss cremini mushrooms, fennel, and garlic with 2 tablespoons extra-virgin olive oil. Roast, stirring once or twice, for 20 minutes. Set aside.

4 In a small saucepan over medium-high heat, bring vegetable stock to a simmer.

5 In a large sauté pan over medium-high heat, heat remaining 2 tablespoons extra-virgin olive oil. Add white and light green parts of scallions, and stir for 1 minute.

6 Add drained farro and white wine, stir until wine is evaporated, and add 1 cup vegetable stock. Cook, stirring, until stock is absorbed.

7 Add remaining 1 cup vegetable stock along with roasted vegetables, and stir until stock is absorbed.

8 Stir in reserved dark green parts of scallions, season to taste with remaining ½ teaspoon kosher salt, and serve.

INGREDIENTS

2 cups farro

1½ tsp. kosher salt

1 (10-oz.; 285g) pkg. small cremini (baby bella) mushrooms, quartered

2 medium bulbs fennel, tops removed, cut into ½-in. (1.25cm) chunks

2 cloves garlic, finely chopped

4 TB. extra-virgin olive oil

2 cups vegetable stock

1 bunch scallions, white and light green parts separated from dark green parts, thinly sliced

½ cup dry white wine

Grains

Grains, both ancient and common, are a great source of protein. In particular, breads made from sprouted grains are a fantastic way to add protein to your favorite veggie sandwich. Some grains can stand in for meat, too, such as seitan, a meat substitute made from wheat gluten.

Couscous

	AMARANTH	BUCKWHEAT	BULGUR	CORN	COUSCOUS	DURUM WHEAT	FARRO	FREEKEH
WHAT iT iS	A seed rather than a grain, it can be found in both cereal and flour forms. Has an earthy and nutty flavor, with a slightly chewy texture like bulgur or quinoa.	A para-cereal, most commonly found as a husked whole grain or flour. The husked whole grain, or kasha, is nutty and earthy tasting.	A nutty, neutral-flavor cereal wheat that's cracked and partially cooked. Available in coarse, medium, and fine (instant) grind.	Sweet and starchy, fresh corn is chewy and dense with a high sugar content. Cornmeal or flour is sweet without being sugary and is creamy in texture.	Made from semolina, couscous is neutral-flavored granules of durum wheat that have been husked and crushed.	The hardest type of wheat, durum has a higher protein content than many other kinds of wheat and is most often found milled in pasta and flour.	Dense, chewy, and nutty farro comprises a group of whole grains (einhorn, emmer, and spelt).	Green wheat that's been dried, roasted, and cracked, resulting in a smoky and nutty grain that look like green bulgur with a chewy texture.
USES	Use as a starchy base for stews; combine with fruit for porridge; or mix with pastry, batter, or dough.	Used in pancakes, breads, and noodles (such as soba).	Is great in salads. Use as you would use brown rice.	Eat fresh, either on or off the cob; mill into a coarse or fine meal or flour for baked goods and tortillas; as polenta; or as grits or posole.	Serve as a starchy side to tagines or grilled vegetables, or stir into cold salads.	Primarily used for making fresh pasta dough but occasionally also for risen breads.	Use interchangeably with barley. Try it in risottos, in any dish you'd use brown rice or barley, or in hot cereals and whole-grain breads.	Make in a rice cooker on the brown rice setting.
GLUTEN FREE	Yes	Yes	No	Yes	No	No	No	No
GOOD SOURCE OF …	Excellent source of complete proteins, with a perfect amino acid balance.	Protein, fiber, antioxidants, B vitamins, magnesium, phosphorus, and potassium.	Protein, fiber, iron, and B vitamins.	Protein, fiber, and iron.	Protein and selenium.	Protein, magnesium, selenium, manganese, and phosphorus.	Protein, fiber, vitamin B₃, and zinc.	Very high protein and fiber content. Manganese, folate, phosphorus, magnesium, and iron.

Amaranth

Corn

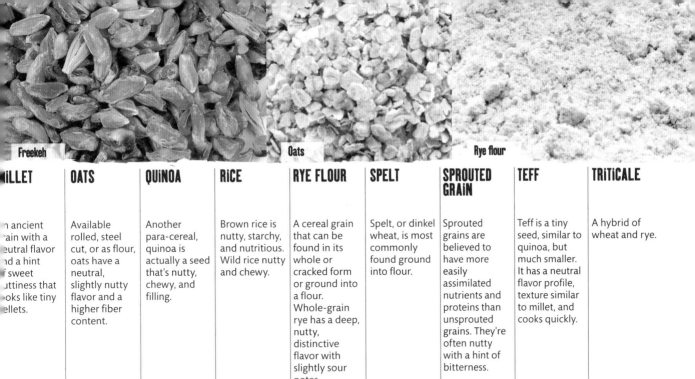

Freekeh   Oats   Rye flour

MILLET	OATS	QUINOA	RICE	RYE FLOUR	SPELT	SPROUTED GRAIN	TEFF	TRITICALE
An ancient grain with a neutral flavor and a hint of sweet nuttiness that looks like tiny pellets.	Available rolled, steel cut, or as flour, oats have a neutral, slightly nutty flavor and a higher fiber content.	Another para-cereal, quinoa is actually a seed that's nutty, chewy, and filling.	Brown rice is nutty, starchy, and nutritious. Wild rice nutty and chewy.	A cereal grain that can be found in its whole or cracked form or ground into a flour. Whole-grain rye has a deep, nutty, distinctive flavor with slightly sour notes.	Spelt, or dinkel wheat, is most commonly found ground into flour.	Sprouted grains are believed to have more easily assimilated nutrients and proteins than unsprouted grains. They're often nutty with a hint of bitterness.	Teff is a tiny seed, similar to quinoa, but much smaller. It has a neutral flavor profile, texture similar to millet, and cooks quickly.	A hybrid of wheat and rye.
Cook as a cereal or prepare like rice.	Cook as a breakfast cereal; use to provide body to veggie burgers and other meat substitutes; or grind into flour for breads, muffins, and other baked goods.	Cook as you would brown rice, or use as a hot cereal.	Enjoy in side dishes, salads, pilafs, and stuffings.	Use it in sourdough breads or breakfast cereals.	Use spelt flour in breads, piecrusts, and sweet baked goods.	Look for sprouted breads, cereals, and pastas.	Use in porridges and stews, as stuffing, or as a pilaf side dish.	Usually found in cereals or some breads.
Yes	Yes	Yes	Yes	No	No.	Varies; see type of grain	Yes	No
Protein, fiber, phosphorus, magnesium, copper, and manganese.	Protein, fiber, thiamin, magnesium, phosphorus, and manganese.	Very high protein and fiber content. Iron, calcium, magnesium, potassium, and zinc.	Protein, fiber, selenium, manganese, magnesium, zinc, and B vitamins.	Protein, fiber, manganese, phosphorus, copper, pantotheic acid, and magnesium.	Protein, fiber, phosphorus, and manganese.	Sprouted grains are a good source of protein and fiber. They're nutritionally comparable to unsprouted grains.	Protein, fiber, iron, and calcium.	Protein, phosphorus, manganese, and iron.

Buckwheat   Millet

Creamy Pasta with Swiss Chard and Tomatoes

This quick and tasty pasta dish couldn't be easier. Swiss chard is chock full of vitamins, and it's a good source of iron, too. The stems are edible, so don't throw them away!

YIELD 8 TO 10 CUPS   SERVING 2 CUPS   PREP 5 MINS   COOK 10 MINS

1   Cook fettuccine in well-salted water according to the package directions.

2   Meanwhile, in a large sauté pan over medium heat, heat extra-virgin olive oil. Add garlic, and cook, stirring, for 30 seconds.

3   Add Swiss chard and kosher salt, and cook, stirring once or twice or until tender. Remove from heat, and cover to keep warm while pasta finishes cooking.

4   When pasta is ready, reserve ½ cup cooking water, and drain pasta. Add pasta to Swiss chard along with tomatoes, sour cream, and crushed red pepper flakes. Toss well, adding a little reserved pasta water if dish seems dry, and serve immediately.

INGREDIENTS

1 lb. (450g) fettuccine

¼ cup extra-virgin olive oil

3 cloves garlic, thinly sliced

1 bunch Swiss chard, washed well and torn into small pieces

½ tsp. kosher salt

2 large tomatoes, cored, seeded, and cut into ¼-in. (.5cm) strips

½ cup plant-based sour cream

½ tsp. crushed red pepper flakes

For quick meals, keep quick-cooking varieties of pasta on hand, such as angel hair or thin spaghetti, which cook in about 3 to 6 minutes.

Whole-Wheat Pasta *e Ceci* (Pasta with Chickpeas) (T) (UNDER 30)

In this easy dish, whole-wheat pasta and chickpeas combine in a spicy tomato sauce that's just brothy enough to eat with a spoon. It's the perfect choice for a fast, filling, nutritious supper.

YiELD 8 CUPS   **SERViNG** 2 CUPS   **PREP** 5 MiNS   **COOK** 20 MiNS

1 Bring a large pot of salted water to a boil over medium-high heat, and cook whole-wheat pasta according to the package directions until *al dente* (fully cooked but still firm to the bite). Drain (do not rinse), and set aside.

2 Meanwhile, in a large saucepan over medium-high heat, heat extra-virgin olive oil. Add sweet onion and kosher salt, and cook, stirring frequently, for about 5 minutes or until onion is softened and translucent. (Adjust heat as necessary.)

3 Stir in garlic and crushed red pepper flakes, and stir for 30 seconds. Stir in tomato paste, and add Italian plum tomatoes with juice and filtered water. Bring to a boil, reduce heat to medium, and cook for 5 minutes.

4 Stir in chickpeas and pasta, and cook for 2 minutes.

5 Stir in white wine and oregano, remove from heat, and serve immediately.

INGREDIENTS

8 oz. (225g) tube-shape whole-wheat pasta, such as chocchiole, or medium shells

3 TB. extra-virgin olive oil

½ large sweet onion, minced (¾ cup)

½ tsp. kosher salt

2 cloves garlic, minced

¼ tsp. crushed red pepper flakes

1 TB. tomato paste

1 (28-oz.; 800g) can peeled Italian plum tomatoes, with juice, lightly crushed by hand

½ cup filtered water or vegetable stock

1 (14.5-oz.; 410g) can chickpeas, rinsed and drained

¼ cup dry white wine

¼ tsp. dried oregano

Crispy, salty, *Toasted Breadcrumbs* are an easy way to enhance dishes like this. In a food processor fitted with a metal blade, process 2 slices whole-wheat bread to coarse crumbs. In a medium nonstick sauté pan over medium heat, stir together breadcrumbs, 1 tablespoon extra-virgin olive oil, $^1/_2$ teaspoon kosher salt, and $^1/_4$ teaspoon freshly ground black pepper until breadcrumbs are golden and evenly toasted. Toss with 1 tablespoon finely chopped fresh Italian flat-leaf parsley, and add to your dish just before serving. Store leftovers at room temperature in a tightly sealed glass jar for up to 7 days.

Swiss Chard Ravioli Ⓣ

Swiss chard and almonds make a creamy and delicious ravioli filling. This recipe uses wonton wrappers for a quick and easy ravioli, but you could use Fresh Pasta Dough instead if you like.

YIELD 40 RAVIOLI   **SERVING** 8 TO 10 RAVIOLI   **PREP** 30 MINS PLUS SOAK TIME   **COOK** 25 MINUTES

1 Soak almonds in cold water for at least 4 hours or overnight.

2 Discard water nuts soaked in, rinse nuts well, and drain.

3 In a large sauté pan over medium-high heat, heat extra-virgin olive oil. Add garlic, and stir for 30 seconds. Add Swiss chard, with water still clinging to leaves, and cook, stirring frequently, for about 10 minutes or until tender. Add water if Swiss chard begins to dry out. Season with kosher salt and black pepper, and cool slightly.

4 In a food processor fitted with a metal blade, process almonds, Swiss chard, lemon juice, and nutritional yeast in pulses until smooth, adding water if necessary to bring mixture together. Cool completely.

5 Place wonton wrappers, a few at a time, on a lightly floured surface. Spoon about 1½ teaspoons filling into center of each wrapper, brush edges of wrappers with water, and pinch edges to seal, pressing out air as you go. (Alternatively, roll Fresh Pasta Dough using a pasta machine or a rolling pin until about $^1/_8$-inch [3mm] thick. Use a 3-inch [7.5cm] round cutter to cut pasta rounds, and fill as directed.)

6 Bring a large pot of salted water to a boil over medium-high heat. Gently drop ravioli into boiling water, and cook for about 3 to 5 minutes or until tender. Serve with your favorite sauce.

INGREDIENTS

½ cup raw almonds

3 TB. extra-virgin olive oil

4 cloves garlic, finely chopped

2 bunches Swiss chard, leaves only, roughly chopped

1 TB. water

½ tsp. kosher salt

¼ tsp. freshly ground black pepper

Juice of ½ lemon (1 TB.)

1 TB. nutritional yeast

1 tsp. water

40 wonton wrappers, or 1 batch *Fresh Pasta Dough*

Swiss chard

Read the ingredients on your wonton wrappers, as many supermarket brands contain eggs. A trip to your local Asian market might be in order to find egg-free wrappers. And don't throw away the Swiss chard stems! Sauté them with garlic and olive oil, and enjoy.

One-Pan Pasta Primavera

This is a "throw everything in one pan" pasta recipe. It's chock full of good-for-you veggies, and afterward, you have only one pan to wash!

YiELD 10 CUPS   **SERViNG** 2 CUPS   **PREP** 10 MiNS   **COOK** 20 MiNS

1 In an extra-large sauté pan with a lid over medium-high heat, heat extra-virgin olive oil. Add yellow onion, and sauté for 2 minutes.

2 Add garlic, spaghetti, vegetable stock, tomatoes with juice, broccoli, carrot, and kosher salt. Bring to a boil, reduce heat to medium-low, cover, and cook for 3 minutes.

3 Uncover, stir, and continue cooking, stirring constantly and adjusting heat as necessary to maintain a brisk simmer, for about 8 minutes or until stock is absorbed and pasta is tender.

4 Stir in baby spinach, peas, and black pepper, toss for 1 minute, and serve immediately.

iNGREDiENTS

¼ cup extra-virgin olive oil

1 medium yellow onion, halved and thinly sliced

2 cloves garlic, thinly sliced

12 oz. (340g) thin spaghetti

4½ cups vegetable stock or water

1 (14-oz.; 400g) can diced tomatoes, with juice

2 cups fresh or frozen broccoli florets

1 medium carrot, peeled, halved, and thinly sliced (½ cup)

1 tsp. kosher salt

1 (5-oz.; 140g) pkg. baby spinach

½ cup fresh or frozen baby peas

½ tsp. freshly ground black pepper

For *Tomato Basil One-Pan Pasta,* omit broccoli, carrot, peas, and spinach, and add a handful of torn fresh basil leaves before serving.

Sesame Noodles

Tahini (sesame paste) and peanut butter combine with tamari sauce, ginger, and garlic in this quick version of a Chinese food classic.

YIELD 8 CUPS   **SERVING** 1 CUP   **PREP** 10 MINS   **COOK** 10 MINS

1   Bring a large pot of water to a boil over medium-high heat. Add kosher salt and linguine, and cook according to the package directions until pasta is tender. Drain, rinse pasta under cold water, and set aside.

2   In a large bowl, whisk together tahini, peanut butter, hot water, tamari, rice vinegar, ginger, toasted sesame oil, and chili garlic sauce.

3   Add cooked linguine, carrot, and English cucumber to sauce. Toss gently, garnish with gomasio and scallions, and serve immediately.

INGREDIENTS

2 tsp. kosher salt

1 lb. (450g) thin linguine

¼ cup tahini

¼ cup creamy peanut butter

¼ cup hot water

2 TB. reduced-sodium tamari or soy sauce

2 TB. rice vinegar

2 TB. grated fresh ginger

1 tsp. toasted sesame oil

1 tsp. chili garlic sauce or Thai chile paste

1 medium carrot, julienne cut

1 English cucumber, julienne cut

3 TB. *gomasio*

¼ cup thinly sliced scallions, light and dark green parts

For a complete *Sesame Noodle Dinner,* add some grilled tofu and a few handfuls of tender Asian greens such as mizuna or tatsoi, garnish with roasted peanuts, and serve.

Tofu, Tempeh, and Seitan

These versatile transition foods provide healthy, flavorful alternatives to meat. Seitan stars in cheesesteaks, gyros, and satay. Sear or stir-fry tofu for a light and healthy protein source, or make some tasty tempeh dishes.

Tofu Summer Rolls

These refreshing tofu and veggie—filled wraps with spicy peanut dipping sauce are really easy to make. They keep nicely in the refrigerator overnight so you can enjoy them for lunch tomorrow.

YIELD 4 (6-INCH; 15.25CM) ROLLS   **SERVING** 1 ROLL   **PREP** 15 MINS PLUS 30 MINS SOAK TIME   **COOK** 3 MINS

1   Place tofu on several layers of paper towels on a cutting board, top with a few more layers of paper towels, place a heavy plate on tofu, and top with a weight such as a large can of tomatoes. Set tofu aside to drain for 30 minutes. Blot dry with paper towels, and cut tofu into ¼-inch (.5cm) strips.

2   In a small nonstick sauté pan over medium-high heat, heat sesame oil. Add tofu, and sear, turning once or twice, for about 2 minutes or until browned on all sides. Drain on paper towels.

3   Soak 1 rice paper wrapper in warm water for 30 seconds, remove from water, and place on your work surface. Quickly line wrapper with 1 lettuce leaf, 2 tablespoons carrot, 2 tablespoons napa cabbage, and ¼ tofu, and sprinkle with 1 tablespoon scallions. Fold short ends of rice paper inward, roll wrapper like a burrito, and press to seal seam. Repeat with remaining rice wrappers and filling. Refrigerate rolls while you make sauce, or overnight.

4   In a small saucepan over medium-low heat, whisk peanut butter, hoisin sauce, lime juice, tamari, and sambal oelek until smooth. Pour into small bowls, and serve hot or cold with rolls.

INGREDIENTS

4 oz. (110g) firm or extra-firm tofu

1 tsp. sesame oil

4 (8-in.; 20cm) rice paper wrappers

4 large leaves soft green leaf lettuce

1 medium carrot, shredded (½ cup)

½ cup shredded napa cabbage

4 or 5 scallions, thinly sliced (¼ cup)

½ cup smooth peanut butter

2 TB. hoisin sauce

Juice of 2 limes (2 TB.)

2 tsp. reduced-sodium tamari

1 tsp. sambal oelek (chili garlic sauce)

For *Vegetable Summer Rolls,* substitute 2 ripe avocados, peeled, seeded, and cut into strips for tofu and skip sautéing. Other delicious filling ideas include cooked rice noodles, sautéed shiitake mushrooms, shredded red cabbage, or thin jicama strips.

Sesame Tofu Cutlets

Tofu cutlets are marinated in ginger, soy, sesame, and garlic and fried crisp with a sesame and breadcrumb crust. They're great with steamed greens and rice, on a salad, or in a sandwich.

YiELD 6 CUTLETS SERVING 2 CUTLETS PREP 2½ HOURS COOK 10 MiNS

1 Cut tofu horizontally into thirds, and cut each third in half. Place tofu on several layers of paper towels, top with more paper towels, set a heavy plate on top, and add a weight. Set aside to drain for 30 minutes.

2 In a large baking dish, whisk together tamari, lemon juice, sesame oil, ginger, and garlic. Add tofu, and refrigerate for 2 hours, turning tofu once or twice.

3 In a small bowl, combine panko breadcrumbs and sesame seeds.

4 Dredge each tofu cutlet in breadcrumb mixture, dip in marinade again, and dredge in breadcrumb mixture a second time to coat well.

5 In a large frying pan over medium-high heat, heat grapeseed oil until oil begins to shimmer. Add tofu cutlets, and fry, turning once and adjusting heat as necessary to prevent burning, for about 3 minutes per side or until golden and crisp.

INGREDiENTS

1 (16-oz.; 450g) pkg. firm tofu

2 TB. reduced-sodium tamari

Juice of 1 lemon (2 TB.)

1 TB. toasted sesame oil

1 TB. grated fresh ginger

2 cloves garlic, finely chopped

½ cup panko breadcrumbs

¼ cup sesame seeds

¼ cup grapeseed oil

For *Sesame Seitan Cutlets*, use seitan instead.

Grilled Tofu Caprese

Silken tofu is grilled with marinated eggplant and stacked with sweet tomatoes and fresh basil.

YiELD 4 STACKS SERVING 1 STACK PREP 30 MiNS COOK 10 MiNS

1 Sprinkle eggplant with ½ teaspoon kosher salt, and set aside on paper towels for 5 minutes. Rinse and pat dry.

2 In a shallow bowl, whisk 2 tablespoons extra-virgin olive oil, garlic, oregano, and 1 tablespoon balsamic vinegar. Add eggplant, and marinate for 15 minutes.

3 Heat a grill to high, or set a grill pan over high heat.

4 Brush tofu with 1 tablespoon extra-virgin olive oil, and sprinkle with a pinch of kosher salt. Add to the grill or grill pan, and cook for about 2 minutes per side or until nicely marked. Brush grill grates with 1 tablespoon olive oil, and grill eggplant for about 3 minutes per side or until tender.

5 Stack 1 slice eggplant, 1 slice beefsteak tomato, 1 slice tofu, 1 basil leaf on each of 4 plates, and repeat. Drizzle with remaining 1 tablespoon olive oil and remaining 2 tablespoons balsamic vinegar, season with black pepper, and serve.

INGREDiENTS

1 small eggplant, skin on, trimmed and cut into 8 even slices

1 tsp. kosher salt

5 TB. extra-virgin olive oil

2 cloves garlic, finely chopped

½ tsp. dried oregano

3 TB. balsamic vinegar

½ lb. (225g) firm or extra-firm tofu, cut into 8 slices

2 large beefsteak tomatoes, each cored and cut into 4 slices

16 large, fresh basil leaves

½ tsp. freshly ground black pepper

ALLIUMS

The allium family includes fragrant bulbs and shoots such as onions, garlic, and leeks. **Benefits** Antibacterial, anti-inflammatory, lowers cholesterol, promotes healthy gut bacteria. **Uses** Choose firm onions and garlic and straight leeks with some "give" to them. Enjoy onions raw in salads and sandwiches or cooked as a flavoring for a variety of dishes. Add garlic to dressings, sauces, marinades, soups, stews, and more. Eat leeks in soups, stews, and savory pies. **Recipes** Caramelized Onions, Summer Squash and Onion Bake, *Pissaladiere,* Potato Leek Soup, Herbed Mushroom and Leek Tart, Stir-Fried Chinese Cress with Fermented Black Beans.

Tofu and Veggie Stir-Fry

I love the clean, bright flavors of this crunchy stir-fry, which uses a ginger vinaigrette to lightly dress seared tofu and fresh vegetables.

YIELD 8 CUPS SERVING 2 CUPS PREP 15 MINS COOK 10 MINS

1 In a small bowl, whisk together soy sauce, sesame oil, rice vinegar, and ginger. Set aside.

2 Heat a large wok or cast-iron skillet over medium heat. When hot, add 1 tablespoon grapeseed oil and garlic, and cook, stirring, for 30 seconds. Add tofu, and cook, stirring, for about 1 minute or until tofu begins to color slightly.

3 Push tofu to the side, add bok choy, and stir for 1 minute.

4 Push bok choy to the side, increase heat to medium-high, and add remaining 1 tablespoon grapeseed oil. Add broccoli, red bell pepper, yellow onion, and shiitake mushrooms, and cook, stirring, for 2 minutes.

5 Add snow peas and water, mix tofu and vegetables, and continue to cook, stirring, for about 2 minutes or until water is nearly evaporated and vegetables are tender.

6 Add reserved dressing, toss, and serve.

INGREDIENTS

1 TB. soy sauce

1 TB. toasted sesame oil

1 TB. rice vinegar

1 TB. finely chopped fresh ginger

2 TB. grapeseed oil

2 cloves garlic, finely chopped

½ lb. (225g) firm or extra-firm tofu, cut in ½-in. (1.25cm) cubes

2 cups thinly sliced bok choy

1 cup small broccoli florets

1 medium red bell pepper, diced in ½-in. (1.25cm) chunks

1 medium yellow onion, diced (¾ cup)

1 cup sliced shiitake mushrooms

1 cup fresh snow peas

¼ cup water or vegetable stock

For *Tofu and Stir-Fried Veggie Dinner,* serve over hot cooked brown rice or rice noodles. For added flavor, sprinkle with cashews.

Hearty Seitan Roast (T)

A simple seitan loaf is browned and then baked in a savory, sweet, and sour sauce with aromatic vegetables for the perfect holiday meal centerpiece dish.

YiELD 1 (1 POUND; 450G) ROAST **SERViNG** ⅙ ROAST AND VEGETABLES **PREP** 15 MiNS **COOK** 30 MiNS

1 Preheat the oven to 375°F (190°C).

2 In a large, preferably cast-iron skillet over medium-high heat, heat 1 tablespoon olive oil.

3 Season Basic Seitan evenly with ½ teaspoon kosher salt and ¼ teaspoon black pepper. Add seitan to the skillet, and brown on all sides, turning every 1 or 2 minutes or until evenly browned.

4 In a small roasting pan, toss yellow onion, carrots, parsnips, and garlic with remaining 1 tablespoon olive oil, herbes de Provence, remaining ½ teaspoon kosher salt, and ¼ teaspoon black pepper. Place browned roast on top of vegetables.

5 In a small saucepan over high heat, whisk vegetable stock, red wine, ketchup, tamari, and balsamic vinegar. Cook, stirring often, for about 10 minutes or until mixture is thickened slightly and reduced to 1 cup liquid. Pour over roast and vegetables.

6 Cover the roasting pan with aluminum foil, and bake for 20 minutes. Uncover, and bake for 10 more minutes.

7 Using a sharp, serrated knife, cut roast into paper-thin slices; place on a serving dish; and spoon some vegetables and sauce over slices. Serve immediately.

iNGREDiENTS

2 TB. olive oil

½ batch *Basic Seitan*

1 tsp. kosher salt

½ tsp. freshly ground black pepper

1 large yellow onion, cut in ½-in. (1.25cm) wedges

2 medium carrots, peeled and cut into 1-in. (2.5cm) chunks

2 medium parsnips, peeled and cut into 1-in. (2.5cm) chunks

2 cloves garlic, thinly sliced

1 tsp. herbes de Provence

1 cup vegetable stock (preferably Basic Seitan cooking stock)

½ cup dry red wine

2 TB. ketchup

1 TB. reduced-sodium tamari

1 TB. balsamic vinegar

For *Seitan Cheesesteak Sandwiches*, heat 1 tablespoon olive oil in a cast-iron skillet over medium-high heat. Add ¼ cup onion and ¼ cup button mushrooms, both sliced paper thin, season with kosher salt and black pepper, and cook, stirring often, for 5 minutes or until veggies begin to brown. Add seitan, and brown evenly for 2 or 3 minutes. Scrape onions, mushrooms, and seitan into a 6-inch (15.25cm) long pile, and cover with 2 slices plant-based cheese. Slice open a 6-inch (15.25cm) sub or hoagie roll, place it over mixture in the pan, and heat for 1 minute. Use a spatula to scrape everything onto roll, and serve.

Tempeh Milanese

Tempeh is breaded, quickly fried, and served with a lemon arugula salad for a meatless take on the classic Italian chicken Milanese.

YiELD 8 CUTLETS PLUS 6 CUPS SALAD **SERVING** 2 CUTLETS PLUS 1½ CUPS SALAD **PREP** 10 MiNS **COOK** 60 MiNS

1 Preheat the oven to 350°F (180°C).

2 Cut tempeh in half horizontally, and cut each piece into 4 equal-size cutlets. Place tempeh in a baking dish large enough to hold it in one layer.

3 In a small bowl, whisk together water, 2 tablespoons lemon juice, tamari, 2 tablespoons extra-virgin olive oil, and garlic. Pour over tempeh, cover the dish tightly with aluminum foil, and bake for 50 minutes. Remove the foil, drain, and cool tempeh slightly.

4 Place Italian-seasoned panko breadcrumbs in a shallow bowl.

5 In a large frying pan over medium-high heat, heat grapeseed oil until it begins to shimmer.

6 Dredge tempeh cutlets in panko, add to the frying pan, and fry, turning once, for about 2 minutes per side or until golden and crisp. (Adjust heat as necessary to prevent burning.)

7 In a large bowl, toss arugula with remaining 2 tablespoons lemon juice and 2 tablespoons extra-virgin olive oil, and season with kosher salt and black pepper.

8 Divide arugula among 4 serving plates, and equally divide grape tomatoes and kalamata olives on top. Top each salad with 2 tempeh cutlets, and serve immediately.

INGREDIENTS

1 (8-oz.; 225g) pkg. tempeh

½ cup water

Juice of 2 lemons (4 TB.)

2 TB. reduced-sodium tamari

4 TB. extra-virgin olive oil

2 cloves garlic, finely chopped

1 cup Italian-seasoned panko breadcrumbs

½ cup grapeseed oil

½ tsp. kosher salt

¼ tsp. freshly ground black pepper

4 cups baby arugula

2 cups grape tomatoes, halved

½ medium red onion, very thinly sliced

¼ cup pitted kalamata olives

Lemons

Can't find Italian-seasoned panko? To make your own, combine 1 cup plain panko with 1 teaspoon dried oregano, ½ teaspoon dried basil, and ½ teaspoon garlic powder.

Seitan and Dumplings (T)

Simple, delicious, cornmeal and herb-spiked batter puffs up into pillowy dumplings that are nestled atop a stew of seitan chunks and tender veggies.

YIELD 12 CUPS   **SERVING** 2 CUPS   **PREP** 25 MINS   **COOK** 40 MINS

1 In a Dutch oven over medium-high heat, heat 1 tablespoon grapeseed oil. Add Basic Seitan chunks in batches, and sauté, stirring gently, for 5 minutes or until browned. Set aside on a plate, and cover to keep warm while you cook remaining seitan.

2 Add remaining 1 tablespoon grapeseed oil to the pan, along with yellow onion, carrots, button mushrooms, celery, 1 teaspoon kosher salt, and ½ teaspoon black pepper. Cook, stirring frequently and adjusting heat as needed to prevent burning, for 5 minutes.

3 In a medium bowl, whisk soy milk with apple cider vinegar. Set aside to curdle slightly.

4 In a large bowl, whisk together 1½ cups all-purpose flour, yellow cornmeal, baking powder, Italian flat-leaf parsley, thyme, Bell's seasoning, remaining 1 teaspoon kosher salt, and remaining ½ teaspoon black pepper. Pour in soy milk mixture, and stir just until combined—do not knead. Set aside for 10 minutes.

5 Add remaining 3 tablespoons all-purpose flour to vegetables, and stir for 1 minute. Add vegetable stock, and stir vigorously to release any browned bits from the bottom of the pan.

6 Stir in seitan and tiny green peas, and bring to a boil. Drop in dumpling batter by the heaping tablespoonful, spacing evenly (you'll have about 10 dumplings, which will cover surface of stew). Cover, reduce heat to low, and cook—*without opening the lid*—for 15 minutes. Uncover, remove from heat, and serve.

INGREDIENTS

2 TB. grapeseed oil

1 loaf *Basic Seitan*, pulled into small chunks before simmering, or 1 (1-lb.; 450g) pkg. seitan pieces

1 large yellow onion, halved and thinly sliced

2 large carrots, peeled and cut into ½-in. (1.25cm) rounds

1 (8-oz.; 225g) pkg. button mushrooms, quartered

2 large stalks celery, cut in ½-in. (1.25cm) slices (1 cup)

2 tsp. kosher salt

1 tsp. freshly ground black pepper

1½ cups soy or hemp milk

1 tsp. apple cider vinegar

3 TB. plus 1½ cups all-purpose flour

½ cup coarse yellow cornmeal

2 TB. baking powder

2 TB. finely chopped fresh Italian flat-leaf parsley

½ tsp. dried thyme

½ tsp. Bell's seasoning or poultry seasoning

5 cups vegetable stock

1 cup fresh or frozen tiny green peas

For light and fluffy dumplings, don't knead the dough; just stir it to combine and then let it rest for 10 minutes so the baking powder can create an airy batter. And don't peek! The steam created inside the pot is what cooks the dumplings. Skip any of these steps, or cheat and peek, and you'll end up with soggy, gummy, leaden dumplings rather than fluffy pillows of cornbread-y dumpling goodness.

Seitan Satay (T)

Skewers of marinated tempeh are grilled or broiled and dipped in tasty peanut-tamarind dressing. Pass these at your next party for rave reviews!

YIELD 8 SKEWERS   **SERVING** 2 SKEWERS   **PREP** 2½ HOURS   **COOK** 10 MINS

1   Place Basic Seitan chunks in a baking dish large enough to hold it in a single layer.

2   In a small bowl, whisk together ¼ cup tamari, water, sesame oil, coconut oil, 1 tablespoon ginger, and garlic. Pour over seitan, and stir well. Cover and refrigerate for 2 hours or overnight.

3   Soak 8 bamboo skewers in warm water for at least 30 minutes. Drain.

4   Preheat a broiler, a grill, or a grill pan for direct cooking over high heat. Brush a broiler pan, grill pan, or grill grates with a light coating of oil.

5   In a medium bowl, whisk tamarind paste with hot water to soften. Add chunky peanut butter, coconut milk, remaining 2 tablespoons ginger, remaining 2 tablespoons tamari, and crushed red pepper flakes, and whisk well.

6   Thread seitan onto skewers, and cook, turning once or twice, for 5 to 7 minutes or until browned on all sides. Serve immediately with tamarind-peanut sauce.

INGREDIENTS

1 loaf *Basic Seitan*, cut into 1-in. (2.5cm) chunks

¼ cup plus 2 TB. reduced-sodium tamari

¼ cup water

1 TB. toasted sesame oil

1 TB. melted coconut oil

3 TB. grated fresh ginger

2 cloves garlic, finely chopped

2 TB. tamarind paste

2 TB. hot (not boiling) water

½ cup chunky peanut butter

½ cup full-fat coconut milk, well shaken

1 tsp. crushed red pepper flakes

Can't find tamarind paste? Use 2 tablespoons brown sugar instead, and eliminate the hot water soak.

Meat Substitutes

You have many options for replacing meat in recipes. Try substituting natural, nutritious, whole foods, such as cooked lentils, for the meat in your favorite taco or chili recipe. Make a burger patty out of beans, or marinate a portobello mushroom and toss it on the grill for a fantastic burger experience. To add a bit more substance, add millet or quinoa to beans and legumes when making meatloaf or burgers.

As the meatless diet becomes more mainstream, your options increase. Your supermarket produce section is likely filled with meat-free offerings, including sausages of all kinds—chorizo, hot dogs, Italian-style sausages, and even Andouille are available at many stores. Deli slices for sandwiches, fake bacon, and meatless burgers of all kinds are available fresh or frozen.

	TOFU	TEMPEH	SEITAN
WHAT IT IS	Made from soy; it has a neutral flavor and soft texture.	Cultured and fermented soy protein; it has a nutty flavor and slightly chewy texture.	Made from wheat gluten; it has a meaty and chewy texture with a similar "bite" to chicken.
USES	Stir-fries, cutlets, soups and stews, grilling, spring rolls, marinated dishes.	Fake bacon, sandwiches, baked dishes, cutlets, marinated dishes.	Soups and stews, grilling, chicken and beef substitute, sandwiches.
GOOD SOURCE OF ...	Protein, calcium, iron, isoflavones.	Protein, calcium, iron, B vitamins (except B_{12}), isoflavones, antioxidants, fiber.	Protein, essential amino acids, vitamin C, niacin, iron, riboflavin.

Tofu

Maple-Glazed Tofu

Enjoy this sweet and savory grilled tofu with a side of Southern-Style Braised Greens and a side of brown rice, or make a sensational sandwich with crisp lettuce, fresh tomato, and a smear of spicy mustard.

YIELD 8 SLICES   SERVING 2 SLICES   PREP 20 MINS   COOK 10 MINS

1   Place tofu on several layers of paper towels, top with more paper towels, set a heavy plate on top, and add a weight. Set aside to drain for 15 minutes.

2   Meanwhile, in a small saucepan over medium-high heat, combine balsamic vinegar, maple syrup, 1 tablespoon extra-virgin olive oil, and tamari. Bring to a boil, and cook, stirring often, for about 10 minutes or until sauce has reduced to a sticky glaze.

3   Preheat a grill or grill pan to high. Brush the grill with remaining 1 tablespoon extra-virgin olive oil.

4   Pat tofu dry with paper towels, brush with glaze, and grill for about 2 minutes per side, turning carefully and brushing with more glaze. Serve immediately.

INGREDIENTS

1 lb. (450g) firm or extra-firm tofu, sliced into 8 slices

¼ cup balsamic vinegar

3 TB. maple syrup

2 TB. extra-virgin olive oil

1 TB. reduced-sodium tamari

Tempeh Bacon

This tempeh bacon is crispy, salty, smoky, and a little sweet. An overnight marinade is best, so if you can, make it the day before you want to use it.

YIELD 12 SLICES   SERVING 2 OR 3 SLICES   PREP 10 MINS PLUS MARINATING TIME   COOK 5 MINS

1   Using a serrated knife, cut thin slices from long end of tempeh. You should be able to get 12 slices (or more) from 1 package. Lay slices in 1 layer in a large baking pan.

2   In a small saucepan over high heat, whisk together water, tamari, maple syrup, apple cider vinegar, brown sugar, smoked sea salt, sesame oil, smoked paprika, and black pepper. Bring to a boil, remove from heat, and pour over tempeh slices. Cover the baking pan, and refrigerate for at least 3 hours or up to 3 days.

3   In a large, heavy, preferably cast-iron frying pan over medium heat, heat grapeseed oil. Allow some marinade to drain from tempeh slices, but do not dry them completely. Discard remaining marinade. Add tempeh slices to pan a few at a time, and cook, turning every 2 minutes, until crispy and browned on both sides, watching carefully to prevent burning. Serve immediately.

INGREDIENTS

1 (8-oz.; 225g) pkg. tempeh

¼ cup water

3 TB. reduced-sodium tamari

2 TB. maple syrup

1 TB. apple cider vinegar

1 TB. brown sugar

2 tsp. smoked sea salt

1 tsp. toasted sesame oil

½ tsp. smoked paprika

½ tsp. coarsely ground black pepper

1 TB. grapeseed oil

Seitan Gyros (T)

Sliced seitan is marinated with traditional Greek flavors of lemon, extra-virgin olive oil, and garlic; grilled until nicely charred; and served on warm pita with all the fixings.

YiELD 6 GYROS   **SERViNG** 1 GYRO   **PREP** 30 MiNS   **COOK** 10 MiNS

1   In a small bowl, whisk together extra-virgin olive oil, lemon juice, Italian flat-leaf parsley, kosher salt, black pepper, and garlic.

2   Slice Basic Seitan loaf very thinly, and place slices in a single layer in a large baking dish. Pour marinade over top, and set aside at room temperature for 25 minutes.

3   Preheat a grill or a grill pan for high-heat direct cooking. Brush grill with a little olive oil.

4   Remove seitan slices from marinade, add to the grill or grill pan, and grill for about 1 minute per side or until charred.

5   Quickly grill pita breads just to warm. Evenly divide seitan among pita, and top with romaine lettuce, plum tomatoes, and red onion. Drizzle each gyro with Tzatziki, sprinkle with sweet paprika, roll, and serve immediately.

iNGREDiENTS

¼ cup extra-virgin olive oil, plus more for grilling

Juice of 2 lemons (¼ cup)

2 TB. finely chopped fresh Italian flat-leaf parsley

1 tsp. kosher salt

½ tsp. freshly ground black pepper

1 clove garlic, crushed and finely chopped

1 loaf *Basic Seitan*

6 pita breads, preferably pocketless

3 cups shredded romaine lettuce

3 plum tomatoes, cored and cut into small dice

½ small red onion, very thinly sliced

1 batch *Tzatziki*, or 1 cup plain, plant-based yogurt mixed with juice of ½ lemon (1 TB.)

1 tsp. sweet paprika

For Seitan Reubens, slice seitan and brush with a few tablespoons soy sauce. Brown in a cast-iron pan with 1 tablespoon oil for 2 or 3 minutes, and pile it on rye bread with ½ cup sauerkraut and ¼ cup plant-based Havarti or cheddar-style cheese per sandwich. In a small bowl, stir together 2 tablespoons plant-based mayo, 1 tablespoon ketchup, and 1 tablespoon sweet pickle relish. Drizzle 1 tablespoon dressing over each sandwich, top with another slice of rye bread, and toast sandwiches in the cast-iron pan over medium heat. Serve immediately with mustard on the side and lots of potato chips.

Breads, Pizzas, and Savory Tarts

Bake your own bread, or prepare a satisfying, savory tart. Pizza—with homemade dough—is here, too. Enjoy!

Easy Slow-Rise Oatmeal Bread

This bread is simple, foolproof, easy to double, and just plain good. It's very adaptable to a working person's schedule; it can rise at room temperature, or for longer periods of time in the refrigerator, and it makes great sandwiches and toast.

YiELD 1 (9-INCH; 23CM) LOAF   **SERViNG** 1 OR 2 SLiCES   **PREP** 10 MiNS PLUS 2 (5 - TO 8-HOUR) RiSES   **COOK** 45 MiNS

1   In a food processor fitted with a metal blade or in a blender, grind rolled oats to a coarse flour.

2   In a large bowl, combine oat flour, 3 cups all-purpose flour, kosher salt, granulated cane sugar, and yeast. Slowly stir in warm water to form a shaggy dough. Sprinkle with an additional 1 or 2 tablespoons all-purpose flour, and knead for 50 turns. Dough will be sticky but cohesive. Place back in the bowl, cover with plastic wrap that's been lightly sprayed with cooking spray, and let rise at room temperature for 6 to 8 hours.

3   Butter or oil a 9-inch (23cm) loaf pan.

4   Punch down dough, knead for 1 or 2 minutes with an additional sprinkling of flour. Shape dough into an approximate loaf form, and fit it into the prepared loaf pan. Cover with plastic wrap or a tea towel, and let rise at room temperature for about 5 more hours or until doubled.

5   About 20 minutes before you want to bake your bread, preheat the oven to 400°F (200°C).

6   Using a sharp knife, slash center of loaf. Brush loaf with nondairy milk, and bake for 45 minutes or until loaf is golden and sounds hollow when tapped on the bottom. Cool completely in the pan on a cooling rack before slicing.

INGREDiENTS

¾ cup rolled oats

3 cups plus 2 or 3 TB. all-purpose flour

1 tsp. kosher salt

½ tsp. granulated cane sugar

½ tsp. active dry yeast

1½ cups very warm (110°F; 43°C) water

1 tsp. nondairy milk

For *Rosemary Raisin Walnut Bread,* steep 1 sprig rosemary in 1 ½ cups hot water. Let water cool to warm, strain, and proceed with recipe as directed, using rosemary water to mix dough. During the first kneading, work in ½ cup raisins and ½ cup toasted, chopped walnuts.

Pizza Dough

There's nothing like the fresh-from-the-oven flavor of homemade pizza. You can top this versatile dough with anything from olive oil and fresh herbs for a simple focaccia, to tomato sauce and your favorite sautéed veggies for a pizza supreme.

YIELD 1 (11×17-INCH; 28×43CM) CRUST **SERVING** ⅛ CRUST **PREP** 15 MINS, PLUS 2 HOURS RISE TIME **COOK** 25 MINS

1 To "proof" yeast, sprinkle it over warm water and set aside for 10 minutes or until foamy.

2 Whisk in extra-virgin olive oil.

3 In a large bowl, combine all-purpose flour and kosher salt. Slowly pour yeast mixture into flour mixture, and use a rubber spatula to gently combine. When dough comes together in a shaggy mass, use your hands to knead dough against the side of the bowl for about 3 minutes, gently pressing it to ensure all flour is incorporated.

4 Cover the bowl with plastic wrap, and set aside to rise in a warm place, such as your unlit oven with the light turned on for about 1 to 1½ hours or until doubled in size.

5 Preheat the oven to 450°F (230°C). Lightly grease a (11×17-inch; 28×43cm) baking sheet.

6 Using a spatula, turn out dough onto the baking sheet. Using floured hands, gently stretch and press dough into the baking sheet until it reaches the corners. Cover dough with oiled plastic wrap, and let rise for another 30 minutes.

7 Gently add toppings to crust, and bake for 25 minutes or until bottom of crust is golden brown.

INGREDIENTS

2½ tsp. active dry yeast

1⅔ cups very warm (110°F; 43°C) water

3 TB. extra-virgin olive oil

4 cups all-purpose flour

1 TB. kosher salt

For *Simple Focaccia,* drizzle dough with extra-virgin olive oil, and top with 1 tablespoon chopped fresh rosemary and ¼ cup pitted, chopped oil-cured olives.

Herbed Mushroom and Leek Tart

Puff pastry is topped with tender, sweet leeks and sautéed mushrooms in this beautiful free-form rectangular tart. Serve it with a salad for a light meal, or cut it into small squares for a party-worthy appetizer.

YiELD 2 (6½x4½-INCH; 16.5x11.5CM) TARTS **SERViNG** ½ TART **PREP** 15 MiNS **COOK** 30 MiNS

1   Preheat the oven to 400°F (200°C). Line a baking sheet with parchment paper.

2   In a large sauté pan over medium heat, heat 2 tablespoons extra-virgin olive oil. Add leeks, and cook, stirring 2 or 3 times, for 10 minutes.

3   Stir nutritional yeast into leeks, transfer to a small bowl, and set aside.

4   Wipe the sauté pan clean, and set over medium-high heat. Add 4 tablespoons olive oil. When hot, add cremini mushrooms, shiitake mushrooms, and garlic, and cook, stirring frequently, for 10 minutes, adding more of remaining 2 tablespoons olive oil if necessary.

5   Stir in kosher salt, black pepper, thyme, chives, and Italian flat-leaf parsley. Remove from heat, and set aside to cool slightly.

6   On a floured surface, roll out puff pastry to a 14×10-inch (35.5×25cm) rectangle. Cut in half crosswise, and transfer both halves to the prepared baking sheet. Fold outer ½ inch (1.25cm) of pastry inward, forming a border, and press to seal tightly. Prick single layer of pastry inside border all over with a fork.

7   Spread leek mixture evenly over pastry, and add mushroom mixture. Bake for 20 minutes or until pastry is puffed and golden. Slice and serve immediately.

INGREDiENTS

8 TB. extra-virgin olive oil

1 bunch leeks, sliced (3 cups)

1 TB. nutritional yeast

1 (6-oz.; 170g) pkg. cremini (baby bella) mushrooms, thinly sliced

1 (6-oz.; 170g) pkg. shiitake mushrooms, stemmed and thinly sliced

2 cloves garlic, finely chopped

½ tsp. kosher salt

½ tsp. freshly ground black pepper

1 TB. chopped fresh thyme

1 TB. minced fresh chives

1 TB. finely chopped fresh Italian flat-leaf parsley

1 sheet puff pastry

Leeks

To make this in a tart pan, line a 10-inch (25cm) tart pan with a removable bottom with ½ recipe Pie Pastry, folding the edges inward. Fill pastry with leek mixture, followed by mushroom mixture. Bake for about 40 minutes or until pastry is golden.

Pissaladiere (Provencal Onion Tart)

Tender dough is piled high with sweet caramelized onions, briny capers, and olives in this Provencal treat. Pissaladiere can be served hot or at room temperature, so if you're making it for a party or picnic, you can prepare it in advance.

YiELD 1 (11x17-iNCH; 28x43CM) TART **SERVING** ⅛ TART **PREP** 90 MiNS **COOK** 30 MiNS

1 In a very large, wide skillet with a lid over medium-high heat, heat extra-virgin olive oil. Add yellow onions all at once, and cook, stirring, for 5 minutes. Cover, reduce heat to low, and cook, stirring occasionally, for 20 minutes.

2 Uncover and cook, stirring 2 or 3 times, for 20 to 30 minutes or until onions have caramelized into a soft, golden mass. Stir in thyme, remove from heat, and set aside to cool slightly.

3 Preheat the oven to 425°F (220°C). Lightly oil a rimmed baking sheet.

4 Roll out Pizza Dough to fit the baking sheet, gently pressing it into the corners. Cover with oiled plastic wrap, and let stand at room temperature for 20 minutes.

5 Remove plastic wrap, spoon onions evenly over dough, scatter capers and Niçoise olives evenly over onions, and bake for about 30 minutes or until crust is golden brown. Serve hot or at room temperature.

INGREDIENTS

2 TB. extra-virgin olive oil

4 lb. (2kg) yellow onions, halved and thinly sliced

2 tsp. fresh thyme leaves

1 batch *Pizza Dough*

2 TB. salted capers, rinsed and drained

30 pitted Niçoise olives

Desserts

Going plant based doesn't mean going without dessert! Whether you're in the mood for a cookie, a pie, or a simple fruit dessert, you'll find plenty here to love.

Pumpkin Pudding Pie

Creamy pumpkin pudding, spiced with a bit of cinnamon and ginger, fills a sweet and salty gingersnap crust for a perfectly homey pudding pie. Tapioca pearls might be a new texture for some, but they're a great way to thicken an eggless custard.

YIELD 1 (10-INCH; 25CM) DEEP-DISH PIE **SERVING** ⅒ PIE **PREP** 10 MINS PLUS COOL TIME **COOK** 30 MINS

1 Preheat the oven to 350°F (180°C).

2 In a food processor fitted with a metal blade, process gingersnap cookies, butter, and 1 teaspoon kosher salt until mixture resembles coarse crumbs. Press mixture into a 10-inch (25cm) deep-dish pie pan, place pie pan on a rimmed baking sheet, and bake for 20 minutes. Remove from the oven, and set aside to cool.

3 Meanwhile, in a medium saucepan, whisk together instant tapioca, cinnamon, ginger, brown sugar, and remaining 1 teaspoon kosher salt. Place the pan on the burner, set the heat to low, and slowly whisk in coconut milk coffee creamer, ½ cup nondairy milk, maple syrup, and vanilla extract. Increase heat to medium, and bring to a boil.

4 In a small bowl, whisk together cornstarch and remaining ½ cup nondairy milk. Whisk cornstarch mixture into tapioca mixture, and continue whisking slowly for about 3 minutes or until mixture is thickened.

5 Whisk in pumpkin purée, remove from heat, and cool for 10 minutes.

6 Pour pumpkin pudding into baked gingersnap crust, spreading with a spatula to smooth top. Cool for 10 minutes, cover with plastic wrap (or invert a large glass bowl over top), and refrigerate overnight. Store leftover pie in the refrigerator for up to 2 days.

INGREDIENTS

10 oz. (285g) gingersnap cookies (about 3 cups broken cookies)

4 TB. melted plant-based butter or coconut oil

2 tsp. kosher salt

¼ cup instant tapioca, such as Minute Tapioca

1 tsp. ground cinnamon

½ tsp. ground ginger

¾ cup brown sugar, lightly packed

1 cup coconut milk coffee creamer

1 cup nondairy milk

1 TB. maple syrup

1 tsp. vanilla extract

¼ cup cornstarch

1 (15-oz.; 420g) can pumpkin purée, or 2 cups fresh pumpkin purée

For *Perfect Pumpkin Pudding,* omit crust, spoon pudding into dessert dishes, cover, and chill. Garnish with crushed gingersnaps or graham crackers or plant-based whipped cream such as CocoWhip.

Apple Crumble Pie ⓣ

The nutty streusel crumble on this pie crowns a filling of tender, sweet, cinnamon-kissed apples. Rather than gummy flour and cornstarch thickeners, instant tapioca is used to thicken and let the pure fruit flavor shine through.

YIELD 1 (10-INCH; 25CM) PIE   **SERVING** ⅛ PIE   **PREP** 25 MINS   **COOK** 60 MINS

1 Preheat the oven to 350°F (180°C).

2 In a food processor fitted with a metal blade, pulse together whole-wheat pastry flour, walnuts, brown sugar, and ½ teaspoon cinnamon to combine. Add butter, and pulse until mixture resembles coarse crumbs. Set streusel topping aside.

3 Roll Pie Pastry for bottom crust into a 13-inch (33cm) circle, and transfer to a 10-inch (25cm) deep-dish pie plate. You'll have a 1-inch (2.5cm) overhang; fold up overhanging dough, pinch into a rim, and use your fingers to crimp crust. Refrigerate crust while you make filling.

4 In a large bowl, whisk together remaining 2 teaspoons cinnamon, granulated sugar, and instant tapioca. Add sliced apples and lemon juice, and toss well to combine. Pour apples into prepared crust.

5 Using your hands, pick up small handfuls of streusel topping, press into large crumbs, and break into smaller crumbs as you sprinkle it over apple filling. Continue, covering top of pie evenly, until all streusel has been used.

6 Bake pie on a rimmed baking sheet in the lower third of the oven for about 1 hour or until streusel topping is golden and filling is bubbly. Check pie once or twice during baking, and place a piece of heavy-duty aluminum foil over top if streusel becomes too brown.

7 Cool pie at room temperature for 3 hours before slicing.

INGREDIENTS

1 cup whole-wheat pastry flour

1 cup walnuts

½ cup brown sugar, lightly packed

2½ tsp. ground cinnamon

4 TB. chilled plant-based butter, cut in small cubes

½ batch *Pie Pastry*, or prepared crust for a single-crust deep-dish pie

¾ cup granulated sugar

1 TB. instant tapioca, such as Minute Tapioca

7 medium apples, such as Granny Smith or Northern Spy, peeled, cored, and thinly sliced (about 2 lb.; 1kg)

Juice of 1 lemon (2 TB.)

Granny Smith apples

I love to bake apple pies with a mix of apples—a majority of crisp baking apples along with one or two "sauce" apples that break down around the slices for a perfect consistency. My favorite sauce apples are Golden Delicious and Ida Red; Northern Spy, Empire, Winesap, and good old Granny Smith are excellent for baking. Ask your local farmer which varieties are best in your region, and have fun mixing it up.

Prairie Berry Pie Ⓣ

This pie, baked in a cast-iron skillet, is bursting with fresh berry flavor, and the superior heat conductivity of cast iron produces a golden, tender bottom crust. Make it with a combination of berries or just a single variety. Try blueberries, raspberries, blackberries, strawberries, or even local, seasonal varieties like huckleberries.

YIELD 1 (10-INCH; 25CM) PIE **SERVING** ⅛ PIE **PREP** 15 MINS **COOK** 70 MINS

1   Preheat the oven to 425°F (220°C).

2   In a large bowl, whisk together light brown sugar, instant tapioca, cornstarch, and kosher salt. Fold in mixed berries, and set aside.

3   Roll Pie Pastry for bottom crust into a 13-inch (33cm) circle, and transfer to a 10-inch (25cm) cast-iron skillet. You'll have a 1-inch (2.5cm) overhang.

4   Pour berry mixture into crust, and spread evenly.

5   Roll dough for top crust into a 12-inch (30.5cm) circle, and carefully lay over top of pie. Trim edges to fit snugly around the inside of the rim of the pan.

6   Fold edges of bottom crust over top crust, and pinch to seal securely. Refrigerate pie for 10 minutes.

7   Crimp edges of chilled crust, using the tines of a fork or your fingers. Cut a hole in center of pie using a small decorative cutter or a sharp paring knife, and cut a few evenly spaced 2-inch (5cm) slits around pie to allow steam to vent during baking.

8   Brush top of pie with nondairy milk, and sprinkle with raw turbinado sugar.

9   Bake on a rimmed baking sheet for 30 minutes, reduce heat to 375°F (190°C), and bake for 40 more minutes. If top crust appears to be browning too quickly (more common in electric ovens), cover loosely with aluminum foil after 30 minutes and then remove the foil for the last 10 minutes of baking time.

10 Cool pie completely at room temperature before slicing—at least 4 hours—to allow filling to set.

INGREDIENTS

1 cup light brown sugar, lightly packed

5 TB. instant tapioca, such as Minute Tapioca

1 TB. cornstarch

½ tsp. kosher salt

7 cups fresh mixed berries, or 3 (12-oz.; 340g) pkg. frozen berries

1 batch *Pie Pastry*, or prepared crust for a double-crust deep-dish pie

1 tsp. nondairy milk

1 tsp. raw turbinado sugar

Crimping pie pastry doesn't just make for a pretty pie; it also secures the top and bottom crusts to ensure the filling won't leak. For a simple, decorative crimp, press one finger into the edge of the crust, and pinch the dough around that finger using your thumb and forefinger. Repeat all around the pie. Chilling the dough after filling the pie makes this process easier.

Blueberry Peach Cobbler

This delightful dish is a fabulous way to showcase summer's finest fruits. The fruit filling mixes with the biscuit topping for a gloriously messy dessert.

YIELD 1 (3-QUART; 3L) COBBLER **SERVING** ⅛ COBBLER **PREP** 15 MINS **COOK** 40 MINS

1 Preheat the oven to 350°F (180°C).

2 Place butter in a 3-quart (3L) cast-iron skillet or casserole dish. Place the pan in the oven until butter is melted.

3 In a large bowl, whisk together cornstarch with ¼ cup sugar. Add peaches, blueberries, cinnamon, and lemon juice, and gently toss with sugar mixture to combine.

4 In a medium bowl, whisk together remaining ¾ cup sugar, all-purpose flour, baking powder, and kosher salt. Stir in coconut milk coffee creamer until mixture forms a rough dough.

5 Remove the skillet from the oven, add peach mixture, and spread to cover bottom of pan. Drop spoonfuls of batter evenly over fruit, and bake on a baking sheet in the lower third of the oven for about 45 minutes. Serve warm.

INGREDIENTS

4 TB. plant-based butter

2 TB. cornstarch

1 cup sugar

1 lb. (450g) fresh peaches, unpeeled, pitted, and sliced

4 cups fresh blueberries

½ tsp. ground cinnamon

Juice of ½ lemon (1 TB.)

1 cup all-purpose flour

2 tsp. baking powder

¼ tsp. kosher salt

1 cup coconut milk coffee creamer

Nutty Berry Streusel Bars

A gorgeous layer of jam peeks out from the coconut-laced streusel that tops these easy-to-make, deliciously crumbly bar cookies. These treats come together in minutes in your food processor.

YIELD 25 BARS **SERVING** 2 BARS **PREP** 10 MINS **COOK** 30 MINS

1 Preheat the oven to 375°F (190°C). Line a 9-inch (23cm) square baking pan with parchment paper or aluminum foil, letting edges overhang several inches. Spray lightly with cooking spray.

2 In a food processor fitted with a metal blade, pulse almond flour, rolled oats, walnuts, all-purpose flour, and sea salt to a coarse meal. Add brown sugar, coconut oil, and butter, and process for about 30 seconds. Reserve 1 cup oat mixture, and press rest into the bottom of the prepared baking pan, packing it tightly. Bake for 10 minutes.

3 Using your fingers, mix coconut into reserved oat mixture. Set aside.

4 Dot baked crust with spoonfuls of blueberry jam, and spread to cover crust. Crumble reserved topping over jam, and bake for 20 more minutes. Cool completely before cutting into bars.

INGREDIENTS

1 cup almond flour

1 cup rolled oats

1 cup walnuts

½ cup all-purpose flour, or gluten-free flour blend

½ tsp. fine sea salt

½ cup brown sugar, lightly packed

½ cup melted coconut oil

2 TB. plant-based butter

¼ cup unsweetened dried coconut

1 cup blueberry, raspberry, or strawberry jam

BERRIES

Blueberries, strawberries, raspberries, blackberries, cranberries, and others are packed with fiber and nutrients. They're delicious eaten raw, baked into desserts, or cooked in sauces. **Benefits** Antibacterial, antioxidant, promote eye health, improve memory, boost urinary tract health, help with digestion, anticancer properties. **Uses** Buy during their peak—spring and summer for most berries and winter for cranberries. Eat fresh as a snack, dessert, or side dish; bake in pies and cakes; or stew as a sauce. **Recipes** Strawberry Muffins, Prairie Berry Pie, Blueberry Peach Cobbler, Berry Streusel Bars, Winter Fruit Compote.

Banana Chocolate-Chip Oatmeal Cookies (T) (UNDER 30)

Chewy, coconutty, and studded with chocolate chips, these cookies are a crowd pleaser and bake sale favorite. Banana is a great plant-based egg substitute when baking and adds a sweet, mild banana flavor.

YIELD 16 COOKIES   **SERVING** 2 COOKIES   **PREP** 15 MINS   **COOK** 12 TO 14 MINS

1   Preheat the oven to 350°F (180°C). Line 2 baking sheets with parchment paper.

2   In a medium bowl, mash banana with granulated sugar, brown sugar, grapeseed oil, and vanilla extract until smooth.

3   Stir all-purpose flour, rolled oats, baking soda, cinnamon, sea salt, bittersweet chocolate chips, and coconut into banana mixture, using your hands to ensure batter is well mixed. It will be very thick.

4   Scoop 1½-inch (3.75cm) balls of dough onto the baking sheets, about 2½ inches (6.25cm) apart. Using wet hands, gently pat down cookies into 2-inch (5cm) rounds. Some chocolate chips might separate from batter—just pat them back into cookies.

5   Bake for 12 to 14 minutes or until cookies are golden. Cool for 3 minutes on baking sheets, and transfer to a wire rack to cool completely. Cookies will keep in an airtight container for up to 5 days (if they last that long!).

INGREDIENTS

1 medium very ripe banana, peeled

⅓ cup granulated sugar

⅓ cup brown sugar, lightly packed

⅓ cup grapeseed oil

1 tsp. vanilla extract

1 cup all-purpose flour

2 cups rolled oats

½ tsp. baking soda

½ tsp. ground cinnamon

¼ tsp. sea salt

½ cup bittersweet chocolate chips

¼ cup unsweetened dried coconut

For *Nutty Banana-Coco-Oat Cookies,* replace coconut with ⅓ cup finely chopped toasted walnuts or pecans—or use both.

Cherry Cheesecake Squares

Sometimes, plant-based food isn't just about being healthy—it's about *dessert*. This dish is messy, delicious, and definitely an indulgence to be enjoyed once in a while.

YiELD 16 SQUARES   SERVING 1 SQUARE   PREP 15 MiNS   COOK 35 MiNS

1 Preheat the oven to 350°F (180°C). Line the bottom of a 9-inch (23cm) square baking pan with aluminum foil, leaving several inches of overhang on each side. Tuck overhang under the edges of the pan, and spray foil with cooking spray.

2 In food processor fitted with a metal blade, pulse chocolate sandwich cookies to fine crumbs. Pulse in butter. Transfer crumb mixture to the prepared baking pan, and press into the bottom of the pan, packing tightly using your hands or the bottom of a drinking glass.

3 In a large bowl, and using an electric mixer fitted with a paddle attachment on medium-high speed, whip soy cream cheese and vanilla soy yogurt until smooth.

4 Beat in confectioners' sugar, vanilla extract, and sea salt.

5 Pour cream cheese mixture over crumb base, and bake for 35 minutes or until set.

6 Spoon cherry pie filling evenly over warm cheese filling, and cool completely. Once cooled, refrigerate for at least 6 hours or overnight before slicing into 16 equal squares.

INGREDIENTS

20 chocolate sandwich cookies

2 TB. plant-based butter, melted

2 (8-oz.; 225g) pkg. soy cream cheese, softened

6 oz. (170g) vanilla soy yogurt

¼ cup plus 1 TB. confectioners' sugar

1 tsp. vanilla extract

Pinch sea salt

1 (21-oz.; 600g) can cherry pie filling

For *Strawberry Cheesecake Squares*, replace chocolate sandwich cookies with about 14 graham crackers, and use 1 pint (470ml) strawberry jam in place of cherry pie filling.

Triple Ginger Molasses Cookies

Fill your cookie jar with these chewy, spicy, molasses and ginger treats, but be warned—they won't last long!

YIELD 24 COOKIES   **SERVING** 2 COOKIES   **PREP** 15 MINS   **COOK** 12 TO 14 MINS

1   Preheat the oven to 350°F (180°C). Line two baking sheets with parchment paper.

2   In a small bowl, whisk raw turbinado sugar and cinnamon, and set aside.

3   In a medium bowl, whisk together whole-wheat pastry flour, ground ginger, baking soda, baking powder, and kosher salt.

4   In another medium bowl, whisk sucanat, grapeseed oil, blackstrap molasses, nondairy milk, and grated ginger until well combined.

5   Stir wet ingredients into dry. When nearly mixed, stir in candied ginger chips. Refrigerate dough for 15 minutes.

6   Scoop up heaping tablespoon-size balls of batter. Roll each ball in cinnamon-sugar mixture, and place 2 inches (5cm) apart on the baking sheets. Bake cookies for 12 to 14 minutes or until golden.

7   Cool cookies on the baking sheets for 2 minutes before transferring to wire racks to cool completely. Store cookies in an airtight container at room temperature for 5 days.

INGREDIENTS

¼ cup raw turbinado sugar

1 tsp. ground cinnamon

2 cups whole-wheat pastry flour

2 TB. ground ginger

½ tsp. baking soda

½ tsp. baking powder

½ tsp. kosher salt

1 cup sucanat

½ cup grapeseed oil

¼ cup blackstrap molasses

¼ cup nondairy milk, such as rice or coconut

1 TB. grated fresh ginger

¼ cup candied ginger chips, or finely diced crystallized ginger

Ginger

Pineapple Cornmeal Upside-Down Cake

In this fun and fabulous retro classic, caramelized pineapple slices are topped with a tender cornmeal batter and then flipped after baking.

YIELD 1 (9-INCH; 23CM) CAKE   **SERVING** ⅛ CAKE   **PREP** 15 MINS   **COOK** 45 TO 50 MINS

1 Preheat the oven to 350°F (180°C). Grease a 9-inch (23cm) round aluminum foil–wrapped springform (or cake pan).

2 In a small bowl, whisk together coconut milk coffee creamer and apple cider vinegar. Set aside to curdle slightly.

3 In another small bowl, whisk together all-purpose flour, yellow cornmeal, baking powder, and kosher salt.

4 In a large bowl, whisk together ¼ cup grapeseed oil, banana, granulated sugar, and vanilla extract until smooth.

5 In a small saucepan over medium-high heat, heat remaining 1 tablespoon grapeseed oil, pineapple juice, and brown sugar. Bring to a boil, stirring constantly, and cook for 1 minute. Pour caramel into the prepared springform pan, and arrange pineapple half-rings over the bottom of the pan in a decorative fashion.

6 Whisk soy milk mixture into wet ingredients, and quickly fold in flour mixture just until incorporated, taking care not to overmix. Pour batter into the pan over pineapple, and smooth with an offset spatula or a spoon dipped in water.

7 Bake for 45 to 50 minutes or until a skewer inserted into center of cake comes out clean and cake springs back when pressed lightly.

8 Run a sharp knife around edge of cake, and cool completely. Unmold sides of pan, carefully flip cake onto a platter, and gently remove bottom of springform, running a thin knife between pineapple and bottom of pan if necessary.

INGREDIENTS

⅓ **cup** coconut milk coffee creamer or soy milk

1 **tsp.** apple cider vinegar

1 **cup** all-purpose flour

¼ **cup** fine yellow cornmeal

2 **tsp.** baking powder

½ **tsp.** kosher salt

¼ **cup plus 1 TB.** grapeseed oil

1 **small ripe banana**, peeled and mashed

½ **cup** granulated sugar

1 **tsp.** vanilla extract

1 **TB.** pineapple juice (reserved from can or fresh pineapple)

2 **TB.** brown sugar

1 **(15-oz.; 420g) can** organic pineapple rings in juice, cut in half, or 1 small fresh pineapple, peeled, cored, and cut into half-rings

This moist, tender cake is easiest to unmold when it's made in a springform pan. If you like, you can place a few maraschino cherries decoratively among the pineapple slices for more vintage recipe fun.

Fudgy Oatmeal Thumbprints

Little cocoa and cinnamon-kissed oatmeal cookies get a fiber boost from walnuts and cacao nibs. They're baked and then filled with a fudgy chocolate ganache center.

YiELD 24 COOKiES   **SERViNG** 2 COOKiES   **PREP** 15 MiNS   **COOK** 12 TO 14 MiNS

1 Preheat the oven to 350°F (180°C). Line 2 rimmed baking sheets with parchment paper.

2 Place flax meal in a small bowl.

3 In a small saucepan over medium heat, heat nondairy milk just until it bubbles around edges. Pour warm milk over flax meal, stir, and set aside for 10 minutes.

4 In a food processor fitted with a metal blade, pulse rolled oats to a coarse meal. Transfer oats to a large bowl, and whisk in all-purpose flour, cocoa powder, baking powder, cinnamon, and kosher salt.

5 In a medium bowl, whisk together coconut oil, brown sugar, and flax mixture vigorously until smooth. Stir into dry ingredients, mixing with a large spatula or wooden spoon to combine. When flour is nearly incorporated, add walnuts and cacao nibs, and mix quickly but thoroughly.

6 Place heaping tablespoon-size balls of dough on the baking sheets about 2½ inches (6.25cm) apart. Pat cookies gently to flatten slightly, and bake for 12 minutes.

7 Remove from the oven, and cool on the baking sheets for 1 minute. Using the handle of a wooden spoon, make an indentation in each cookie. (Be gentle—cookies are crumbly.) Let cool for another minute, and use your thumb to increase size of indentation. Transfer cookies to a wire rack to cool.

8 While cookies are cooling, place chocolate chips in a small, heatproof bowl.

9 In a small saucepan over medium-high heat, heat coffee creamer until hot and just beginning to bubble around edges. (Do not boil.) Pour creamer over chocolate chips, and let stand for 5 minutes. Whisk until smooth, whisk in maple syrup, and let ganache stand for 5 more minutes to firm slightly.

10 Fill indentation in each cookie with ganache. (I use a teaspoon-size cookie scoop to make this task neat and easy.) Cool completely to allow ganache to set up before serving. Cookies will keep, refrigerated, for 3 days.

> For *Fruity Oatmeal Thumbprints*, use fruit jam instead of chocolate to fill cookies. Just bake as directed, cool, and fill indentations with jam instead of chocolate.

INGREDiENTS

2 TB. flax meal (ground flaxseeds)

½ cup nondairy milk, such as almond

1 cup rolled oats

1 cup all-purpose flour

1 TB. unsweetened cocoa powder

2 tsp. baking powder

½ tsp. ground cinnamon

½ tsp. kosher salt

½ cup melted coconut oil

½ cup brown sugar, lightly packed

½ cup finely chopped walnuts

1 TB. raw cacao nibs

¾ cup finely chopped bittersweet chocolate or chocolate chips

¼ cup plant-based coffee creamer

1 tsp. maple syrup

Walnuts

Pumpkin Gingerbread Cupcakes with Cinnamon Frosting (T)

Spicy pumpkin cupcakes are accented with plenty of ginger and toasted pecans and topped with a creamy, fluffy frosting.

YiELD 18 CUPCAKES   **SERViNG** 1 CUPCAKE   **PREP** 20 MiNS   **COOK** 25 TO 35 MiNS

1 Preheat the oven to 350°F (180°C). Line 18 muffin cups with paper liners, or grease with baking spray.

2 In a small bowl, whisk together ½ cup coconut milk coffee creamer and apple cider vinegar. Set aside to curdle slightly.

3 In a large bowl, whisk together all-purpose flour, 1 teaspoon cinnamon, ginger, baking soda, baking powder, kosher salt, nutmeg, and cloves.

4 In a medium bowl, whisk together pumpkin, dark brown sugar, grapeseed oil, and 1 teaspoon vanilla extract until well combined. Whisk in creamer mixture, and stir wet ingredients into flour mixture, mixing well by hand just until smooth. Reserve 2 tablespoons pecans for garnish, and quickly fold rest into batter.

5 Scoop cupcake batter into the prepared tins, filling each halfway and smoothing batter gently with the back of a wet teaspoon. Bake for 25 minutes or until cupcakes spring back when gently pressed. (To make a 9-inch [23cm] square cake, grease pan and bake at 350°F [180°C] for about 35 to 40 minutes or until cake springs back when lightly pressed in the center.) Cool completely before frosting.

6 Meanwhile, in a large bowl and using an electric mixer on medium-high speed, whip butter and soy cream cheese until well combined with no lumps. Sift in confectioners' sugar and remaining 1 teaspoon cinnamon, about 1 cup at a time, beating well between each addition. Beat in remaining 2 tablespoons coconut milk coffee creamer and remaining 1 teaspoon vanilla extract. Refrigerate for about 30 minutes to firm slightly.

7 Generously frost each cupcake, and garnish with reserved pecans. (For a cake, frost or simply sprinkle with confectioners' sugar and pecans and cut into 2-inch [5cm] squares.) Serve immediately, or refrigerate for up to 2 days.

Have fun frosting your cupcakes! Fit a pastry bag with a plain, large round tip, and swirl a big cloud of fluffy frosting onto each cupcake. For a perfect pipe, gently press the pastry bag to move the frosting to the tip and remove any air bubbles. Holding the bag at a slight angle, squeeze gently from the top as you swirl the icing from the outer edge in.

INGREDiENTS

½ cup plus 2 TB. coconut milk coffee creamer

½ tsp. apple cider vinegar

1½ cups all-purpose flour

2 tsp. ground cinnamon

1 tsp. ground ginger

¾ tsp. baking soda

½ tsp. baking powder

½ tsp. kosher salt

¼ tsp. ground nutmeg

Pinch ground cloves

1 (15-oz.; 420g) can canned pumpkin

1 cup dark brown sugar, lightly packed

⅓ cup grapeseed oil

2 tsp. vanilla extract

½ cup pecans, toasted and finely chopped

¼ cup plant-based butter, cut into chunks

¼ cup soy cream cheese

3½ cups confectioners' sugar

Parsnip Cupcakes with Sour Cream Icing

These cupcakes are like carrot cake, but more interesting. They're tasty as well as pretty to look at when topped with a lightly sweetened sour cream icing, but they're equally wonderful when simply dusted with a little confectioners' sugar.

YiELD 12 CUPCAKES   **SERViNG** 1 CUPCAKE   **PREP** 15 MiNS   **COOK** 22 TO 25 MiNS

1   Preheat the oven to 350°F (180°C). Line a 12-cup muffin tin with paper liners.

2   In a small saucepan over medium heat, heat nondairy milk just until it begins to bubble around edges.

3   Place flax meal in a small bowl, pour warm milk over top, stir, and set aside for 10 minutes.

4   In a large bowl, whisk together all-purpose flour, baking powder, kosher salt, cinnamon, and cardamom.

5   Whisk in flax mixture, brown sugar, grapeseed oil, and 1 teaspoon vanilla extract until smooth. Stir into dry ingredients until just combined.

6   Fold in parsnips and currants.

7   Fill each muffin cup just over half full with batter, and bake for 22 to 25 minutes until center of each cupcake springs back and a tester (such as a toothpick or skewer) comes out clean. Cool cupcakes in the pan for 5 minutes and then remove to a wire rack to cool completely.

8   Meanwhile, in a medium bowl and using an electric mixer on medium speed, cream butter and confectioners' sugar until smooth. Quickly beat in sour cream just until smooth.

9   Spread a little icing on each cooled cupcake, or dip cupcakes into icing for a rustic look. Serve immediately. Unfrosted cupcakes will keep in the refrigerator for up to 2 days.

INGREDIENTS

6 TB. nondairy milk, such as soy or rice

2 TB. flax meal (ground flaxseeds)

1 cup all-purpose flour

1½ tsp. baking powder

½ tsp. kosher salt

½ tsp. ground cinnamon

½ tsp. ground cardamom

¾ cup brown sugar, lightly packed

⅔ cup grapeseed oil

1 tsp. vanilla extract

2 medium parsnips, peeled and grated (2 cups)

¼ cup currants

¼ cup plant-based butter

1 cup confectioners' sugar, sifted twice

½ cup plant-based sour cream

Cardamom tastes best when it's ground fresh, so I stock a small jar of whole cardamom pods for my tea rather than ground, which would go stale before I could use it all. To use whole pods in this recipe, lightly crush 5 or 6 pods with a mortar and pestle, remove seeds from outer shell, discard shells, and crush seeds with a tiny pinch of salt to yield ½ teaspoon ground cardamom.

Baking Substitutions

Baking without eggs and butter is easier than you might think, and one look at the dessert recipes in this part shows you won't be missing out on anything when following a plant-based diet. Here are some helpful substitution hints for baking without eggs and dairy products.

Plant-based butter

REPLACE ...	EGGS			EGG WHITES	BUTTER			
WITH ...	Flax	Banana	Applesauce	Agar flakes	Plant-based butter	Non-hydrogenated shortening	Coconut oil	Grapeseed or olive oil
AMOUNT	1 egg = 1 tablespoon flax meal and 3 tablespoons warm water	1 egg = 1 medium, ripe mashed banana	1 egg = ¼ cup applesauce	1 egg white = 1 tablespoon agar flakes plus 1 tablespoon water	1 cup butter = 1 cup plant-based butter	1 stick butter = ½ cup shortening plus 1 tablespoon water	1 cup butter = 1 cup coconut oil plus 1 tablespoon water	1 cup butter = ¼ cup plus 2 tablespoons oil
USES	Whisk together flax meal and warm water, and let stand 15 minutes before using.	Use in chewy recipes, such as cookies.	Use in quick breads and cakes for lower-fat baking.	Whisk together agar flakes and water, refrigerate for 5 minutes, and use immediately.	Use the same as butter. Do not attempt to brown in a recipe that calls for browned butter.	Use sparingly. Provides structure to recipes where butter is creamed with sugar as well as frosting recipes.	Coconut oil is soft-solid and scoopable at room temperature and firm-solid when chilled. Use solid to cream with sugar in recipes that call for butter or melted in recipes that call for oil.	Use in cake, cookie, and quick bread recipes. Add to wet ingredients.

Flaxseeds

Bananas

Almond milk

Coconut

MiLK			BUTTERMiLK	HALF-AND-HALF OR LiGHT CREAM	EVAPORATED MiLK	HEAVY CREAM	HONEY	SUGAR PROCESSED WiTH BONE CHAR
Soy, hemp, or coconut milk beverage	Rice milk	Almond milk	Plant-based milk plus apple cider vinegar or lemon juice	Coconut milk coffee creamer	Canned coconut milk	Cream from canned coconut milk	Agave nectar, maple syrup, or vegan honey substitute	Beet sugar, unprocessed sugar
1 cup milk = 1 cup soy, hemp, or coconut milk	1 cup milk = ¾ cup plus 1 tablespoon rice milk	1 cup milk = 1 cup almond milk	1 cup buttermilk = 1 cup soy, hemp, or coconut milk beverage plus 2 teaspoons apple cider vinegar or lemon juice	1 cup = 1 cup	1 cup = 1 cup	1 cup = 1 cup	1 cup = 1 cup	1 cup = 1 cup
Substitute at a 1:1 ratio in any recipe.	Rice milk is thinner than other plant-based milks, so reduce the quantity by 1 tablespoon.	Use when a nutty flavor is desired.	Whisk together and let stand for 10 minutes to curdle and thicken.	Substitute in any recipe.	Shake can well at room temperature to combine before measuring.	Refrigerate coconut milk until well chilled. Remove thick, solid "cream" at top of can, and use as a substitute for cream.	Substitute in any recipe.	Look for sugar labeled "vegan" or "un-bleached" to avoid sugar processed with bone char, an animal product.

Oils

Maple syrup

Green Apple Sorbet

Fresh apple juice and a simple syrup of sugar and water are all you need to make this refreshing sorbet. Ascorbic acid (vitamin C) keeps the apple juice from turning an unappetizing shade of brown. Find it in the canning section of your supermarket, or ask for it at the pharmacy.

YiELD 4 TO 6 CUPS **SERViNG** ½ CUP **PREP** 10 MiNS **COOK** 5 MiNS

1 In an electric juicer, juice Granny Smith apples. Stir in ascorbic acid, and measure out exactly 6 cups juice.

2 In a small saucepan over medium heat, combine sugar and water. Cook, stirring, for 8 minutes or until sugar is completely dissolved.

3 Stir sugar mixture into apple juice, and mix well.

4 Add vodka (if using) to slow the formation of crystals during freezing, which results in a smoother sorbet. Chill for at least 2 hours.

5 Freeze sorbet in an ice-cream maker according to the manufacturer's instructions. Serve immediately for soft sorbet, or pack into a 1-quart (1L) container and freeze completely. Sorbet will keep in the freezer for 1 month.

INGREDIENTS

7 large Granny Smith apples

½ tsp. ascorbic acid

2/3 cup sugar

1/3 cup water

1 TB. vodka (optional)

For Apple Cider Sorbet, simmer 6 cups unpasteurized apple cider with 1 (3- or 4-inch; 7.5 to 10cm) cinnamon stick and ⅔ cup sugar. Remove cinnamon stick, and stir in vodka (if using). Chill for at least 2 hours, and freeze in an ice-cream maker. For Melon Sorbet, make sugar syrup as directed. Purée 4 cups chopped honeydew, cantaloupe, or watermelon, and combine with sugar syrup and 1 tablespoon lemon juice. Chill and freeze as directed. For Strawberry Sorbet, purée 4½ cups fresh strawberries, press through a mesh strainer to remove seeds, and proceed as directed for Melon Sorbet.

Chunky Applesauce

A mix of tart and sweet apples, plus apple cider, cinnamon, and just a hint of sugar, makes a refreshing applesauce that's perfect at any time of the day.

YiELD 3 TO 4 CUPS **SERVING** 1 CUP **PREP** 10 MiNS **COOK** 45 MiNS

1 In a medium saucepan over high heat, bring tart apples, sweet apples, apple cider, granulated cane sugar, and cinnamon stick to a boil.

2 Reduce heat to medium-low, and cook, stirring occasionally, for 45 minutes or until apples are easily broken down into a rough sauce when stirred.

3 Cool slightly, and remove cinnamon stick. Serve warm, or refrigerate for 2 hours to chill completely. Applesauce will keep in a tightly sealed jar in the refrigerator for up to 1 week.

INGREDiENTS

3 large, tart apples, such as Winesap or Granny Smith, peeled, cored, and chopped

3 large, sweet apples, such as Golden Delicious, peeled, cored, and chopped

1½ cups apple cider

¼ cup granulated cane sugar

1 (3- or 4-in.; 7.5 to 10cm) cinnamon stick

Cinnamon sticks

For Smooth Applesauce, core apples but do not peel. Cook as directed, cool completely, and run through a food mill to purée and remove apple skins.

Winter Fruit Compote

Fresh, seasonal apples and pears combine with dried fruits for a sweet, nourishing, fiber-rich treat. Try this compote with plant-based ice cream or cake for dessert, or spoon onto oatmeal, granola, or yogurt for breakfast. For a holiday treat, serve it in place of cranberry sauce with savory dishes.

YiELD ABOUT 3½ CUPS   **SERViNG** ½ CUP   **PREP** 10 MiNS   **COOK** 25 MiNS PLUS REST/COOL TiME

1. In a large saucepan with a tight-fitting lid over high heat, combine apple cider, dark rum, vanilla bean, cinnamon stick, lemon peel, and granulated cane sugar. Bring to a boil, stirring frequently to dissolve sugar.

2. Stir in tart apple and Bartlett pear, reduce heat to low, and cook, covered, for 10 minutes.

3. Uncover and stir in apricots, figs, raisins, cranberries, and cherries. Cover and cook for 15 minutes or until fruit is soft.

4. Set aside to cool for 1 hour to allow flavors to blend and then remove vanilla bean and cinnamon stick.

5. Refrigerate in an airtight container for about 2 hours or until chilled, and serve. Compote will keep in the refrigerator in an airtight container for 1 week.

INGREDIENTS

1 cup apple cider

2 TB. dark rum

1 vanilla bean, split lengthwise

1 (3- or 4-in.; 7.5 to 10cm) cinnamon stick

2 (2-in.; 5cm) strips lemon peel, thinly sliced

½ cup granulated cane sugar

1 medium tart apple, such as Granny Smith, peeled, cored, and chopped

1 ripe Bartlett pear, peeled, cored, and chopped

½ cup dried apricots, roughly chopped

½ cup dried figs, roughly chopped

½ cup raisins

½ cup dried cranberries

½ cup dried tart cherries

Pears

You can easily change this recipe based on your tastes and the fruit you have on hand. Dried prunes, apples, pears, and candied ginger are all lovely additions or substitutions. When oranges are in season, replace the lemon peel with orange peel, the chopped apple with fresh orange segments, and the apple cider with freshly squeezed orange juice. Vary the spices with star anise or cardamom, or use port wine or brandy in place of the rum.

Cranberry Poached Pears

Sweet pears are cooked in pear nectar with dried cranberries and spices for a naturally sweetened, light, and refreshing autumn or winter dessert with a gorgeous, rosy glow. Choose pears on the firm side of ripe for best results.

YiELD 6 PEARS   SERViNG 1 PEAR PLUS SAUCE AND CRANBERRiES   PREP 15 MiNS   COOK 35 MiNS

1   In a saucepan just large enough to hold pears, stir together pear nectar, cranberry juice, and cranberries.

2   Using a double thickness of cheesecloth, wrap cinnamon stick, cardamom pods, and star anise pod. Pull cheesecloth up into a pouch, and tie with kitchen twine. Add to the saucepan, and set over medium-high heat.

3   Peel pears, leaving stems intact, and cut a small slice off bottoms to allow pears to stand upright. Immediately place pears into pear nectar mixture. When mixture comes to a boil, cover, reduce heat to low, and cook at a gentle simmer for 30 minutes or until pears are easily pierced with a fork.

4   Transfer pears to a serving dish. Remove and discard spice bag.

5   Increase heat under saucepan to high, and cook sauce, stirring frequently, until reduced by half (about 1 cup liquid). Pour sauce over pears, and cool completely.

6   Serve pears at room temperature, or refrigerate and serve chilled. Place 1 pear on each plate, and spoon a few tablespoons sauce and cranberries over top. Pears will keep, covered, in the refrigerator for up to 7 days.

INGREDiENTS

2 cups pear nectar or juice

¼ cup cranberry juice

1 cup dried cranberries

1 (3- or 4-in.; 7.5 to 10cm) cinnamon stick

2 cardamom pods, cracked with a heavy knife

1 star anise pod

6 medium pears

Bosc, Comice, and Bartlett pears are all excellent choices for poaching because they hold their shape when cooked. For a miniature dessert, use 12 tiny Forelle pears instead.

Index

About the Author

Trish Sebben-Krupka is a chef, culinary educator, cookbook author, and freelance editor. She is the owner of Local Girl Makes Food, a personal chef and culinary education business catering to clients interested in vegan, vegetarian, and eco-friendly diets. She is the author of *The Complete Idiot's Guide® Greens Cookbook* and *Idiot's Guides®: Canning and Preserving* and contributor to *The Best of Vegan Cooking*. Trish took her Master Food Preserver training through the Cornell Cooperative Extension and is passionate about home food preservation, sustainable eating, bread baking, and vegetable cuisine. She lives in New Jersey with her husband, Jim, and an assortment of former junkyard cats. Visit her online at trishkrupka.com.

Acknowledgments

Many thanks are due to those who helped make this book possible: very special thanks to the wonderful editorial team at DK, especially Acquisitions Editor Lori Cates Hand and Development Editor Christy Wagner. Thanks also are due to my agent, Marilyn Allen, of the Allen O'Shea Literary Agency, and to Carolyn Doyle, for her careful testing of each recipe in this book. My endless thanks to Nigel Wright for the art direction and design of this beautiful book, and for spending a week with us directing the photo shoots. Thanks to photographer Kevin Bertolacci for the gorgeous photos, and for being such a kind, wonderful soul, and to Food Stylist Laura Kinsey-Dolph for making each dish look perfect and being an absolute joy to cook with. A million thanks to my amazing friends who helped me in the kitchen during the shoots, especially Tamara Cook, Joe Malone, Katlin Andersen (and Baby Jack), and Gina Hyams. Thanks as well to my "volunteer taste-testers," especially my niece, Rebecca Doherty, my siblings Kristin and Rob, and my clients, Alex and Jay, whose feedback was essential to making these recipes perfect for the omnivore's palate. A special debt of gratitude goes to my husband, Jim, whose love and unwavering support know no bounds. This book is for you.

Photo Credits